THE ANXIETY OF INFLUENCE

The Anxiety of Influence

A THEORY OF POETRY

SECOND EDITION

Harold Bloom

New York   Oxford
OXFORD UNIVERSITY PRESS
1997

Oxford University Press

Oxford   New York
Athens   Auckland   Bangkok   Bogotá   Bombay
Buenos Aires   Calcutta   Cape Town   Dar es Salaam
Delhi   Florence   Hong Kong   Istanbul   Karachi
Kuala Lumpur   Madras   Madrid   Melbourne
Mexico City   Nairobi   Paris   Singapore
Taipei   Tokyo   Toronto

and associated companies in
Berlin Ibadan

Library of Congress Cataloging-in-Publication Data
Bloom, Harold
The anxiety of influence : a theory of poetry / by Harold Bloom.
2nd ed.
p.   cm.
ISBN-13 978-0-19-511221-4

1. Poetry. I. Title.
PN1031.B53   1996
809.1—dc20   96-19988

There were 18 printings of the first edition of this book.

Since this page cannot legibly accommodate the acknowledgments, the following
page constitutes an extension of the copyright page.

20 19 18 17 16 15 14 13

Printed in the United States of America

For William K. Wimsatt

CONTENTS

PREFACE

The Anguish of Contamination

I

Most of the first draft of what became *The Anxiety of Influence* was written in the summer of 1967. Revised during the next five years, the little book was published in January 1973. For more than twenty years, I have been bemused by the book's reception, which remains ambivalent. Rather than attempt an explication, this new preface seeks to clarify and enlarge my vision of the influence process, which is still a dark ground in most areas, whether in the high arts, the intellectual disciplines, or the public sphere. Heidegger, whom I cheerfully abhor, nevertheless sets me an example when he says that it is necessary to think one thought and one thought only, and to think it through to the end. There is no end to "influence," a word which Shakespeare used in two different but related senses. Just before the second entrance of the Ghost, in the first scene of *Hamlet*, the scholar Horatio evokes the world of Shakespeare's *Julius Caesar*, where:

A little ere the mightiest Julius fell,
The graves stood tenantless and the sheeted dead
Did squeak and gibber in the Roman streets.
As stars with trains of fire, and dews of blood,
Disasters in the sun; and the moist star
Upon whose influence Neptune's empire stands
Was sick almost to doomsday with eclipse.

Shakespeare may be thinking back two years, to 1598, when he was at work upon Falstaff's last stand in *Henry IV, Part Two*, in an England much troubled by the melancholy of one solar and two lunar eclipses, prompting prognostications of doomsday in 1600. Hamlet, rather than the Last Judgment, marked that year for Shakespeare, but Horatio, more an antique Roman than a Dane, still broods on the "disasters in the sun," reminding us of the starry theory of influence upon those ill-starred, and the moon's (that moist star) influx upon the waves. The flowing from the stars upon our fates and our personalities is the prime meaning of "influence," a meaning made personal between Shakespearean characters. Shakespeare also uses the word "influence" to mean "inspiration," both in the sonnets and in the plays. The sonnet that influenced me in *The Anxiety of Influence* and its sequel, *A Map of Misreading*, I deliberately refrained from citing in either book:

Farewell, thou art too dear for my possessing,
And like enough thou know'st thy estimate;
The charter of thy worth gives thee releasing;
My bonds in thee are all determinate.
For how do I hold thee but by thy granting,
And for that riches where is my deserving?
The cause of this fair gift in me is wanting,
And so my patent back again is swerving.
Thyself thou gav'st, thy own worth then not knowing,
Or me, to whom thou gav'st it, else mistaking,
So thy great gift, upon misprision growing,

Comes home again, on better judgment making.
Thus have I had thee as a dream doth flatter:
In sleep a king, but waking no such matter.

"Swerving" and "misprision" both depend upon "mistaking" as an ironical over-esteeming or over-estimation, here in Sonnet 87. Whether Shakespeare ruefully is lamenting, with a certain urbane reserve, the loss of the Earl of Southampton as lover, or as patron, or as friend, is not (fortunately) a matter upon which certitude is possible. Palpably and profoundly an erotic poem, Sonnet 87 (not by design) also can be read as an allegory of any writer's (or person's) relation to tradition, particularly as embodied in a figure taken as one's own forerunner. The speaker of Sonnet 87 is aware that he had been made an offer that he could not refuse, which is a dark insight into the nature of authentic tradition. "Misprision" for Shakespeare, as opposed to "mistaking," implied not only a misunderstanding or misreading but tended also to be a punning word-play suggesting unjust imprisonment. Perhaps "misprision" in Shakespeare also means a scornful underestimation: either way, he took the legal term and gave it an aura of deliberate or willful misinterpretation. "Swerving," in Sonnet 87, is only secondarily a returning; primarily it indicates an unhappy freedom.

I excluded Shakespeare from *The Anxiety of Influence* and its immediate sequels because I was not ready to meditate upon Shakespeare and originality. One cannot think through the question of influence without considering the most influential of all authors during the last four centuries. I sometimes suspect that we really do not listen to one another because Shakespeare's friends and lovers never quite hear what the other is saying, which is part of the ironical truth that Shakespeare largely invented us. The invention of the human, as we know it, is a mode of influence far surpassing anything literary. I cannot improve upon Emerson's account of this influx. "Shakespeare; Or, the Poet" in *Representative Men* (1850) remains unique in its accurate estimate of the centrality of the poet, then and now:

Shakspeare is as much out of the category of eminent authors, as he is out of the crowd. He is inconceivably wise; the others, conceivably. A good reader can, in a sort, nestle into Plato's brain, and think from thence; but not into Shakspeare's. We are still out of doors. For executive faculty, for creation, Shakspeare is unique. No man can imagine it better. He was the farthest reach of subtlety compatible with an individual self,—the subtilest of authors, and only just within the possibility of authorship. With this wisdom of life, is the equal endowment of imaginative and of lyric power. He clothed the creatures of his legend with form and sentiments, as if they were people who had lived under his roof; and few real men have left such distinct characters as these fictions. And they spoke in language as sweet as it was fit. Yet his talents never seduced him into an ostentation, nor did he harp on one string. An omnipresent humanity coördinates all his faculties. Give a man of talents a story to tell, and his partiality will presently appear. He has certain observations, opinions, topics, which have some accidental prominence, and which he disposes all to exhibit. He crams this part, and starves that other part, consulting not the fitness of the thing, but his fitness and strength. But Shakspeare has no peculiarity, no importunate topic; but all is duly given; no veins, no curiosities: no cowpainter, no bird-fancier, no mannerist is he: he has no discoverable egotism: the great he tells greatly; the small, subordinately. He is wise without emphasis or assertion; he is strong, as nature is strong, who lifts the land into mountain slopes without effort, and by the same rule as she floats a bubble in the air, and likes as well to do the one as the other. This makes that equality of power in farce, tragedy, narrative, and lovesongs; a merit so incessant, that each reader is incredulous of the perception of other readers.

"We are still out of doors" is the crucial sentence there, as Emerson slyly reminds us of the etymology of the word "foreign," which in Shakespeare means "not of one's own household," hence out of doors. I cannot think, at this bad moment, of a better way to see Shakespeare, since the entire movement of our current School of Resentment is towards eradicating Shakespeare's uniqueness. Neo-Marxists, New Feminists, New Historicists, French-influenced theorists all demonstrate their cultural materialism by giving us a reduced Shakespeare, a pure product of the "social energies" of the English Renaissance. My own favorite joke about this is to add to Lacan, or "French Freud," and Derrida, or "French Joyce," the ultimate triumph of what calls itself "theory": Foucault, or "French Shakespeare." The French have never valued originality, and until a belated Romanticism came to France, they never much cared for Shakespeare's plays. They still esteem Shakespeare rather less than do the Indonesians or the Japanese or the Americans. Real multiculturalists, all over the globe, accept Shakespeare as the one indispensable author, different from all others in degree, and by so much that he becomes different in kind. Shakespeare, as I have argued at length elsewhere, quite simply not only is the Western canon; he is also the world canon. That his appeal is equal to audiences of all continents, races, and languages (always excluding the French) seems to me an absolute refutation of our currently fashionable views, prevalent particularly in Britain and America, that insists upon a Shakespeare culture-bound by history and society. As Emerson rightly concluded, no context, not even the theatrical, confines Shakespeare:

> Some able and appreciating critics think no criticism on Shakspeare valuable, that does not rest purely on the dramatic merit; that he is falsely judged as poet and philosopher. I think as highly as these critics of his dramatic merit, but still think it

secondary. He was a full man, who liked to talk; a brain exhaling thoughts and images, which, seeking vent, found the drama next at hand. Had he been less, we should have had to consider how well he filled his place, how good a dramatist he was,— and he is the best in the world. But it turns out, that what he has to say is of that weight, as to withdraw some attention from the vehicle; and he is like some saint whose history is to be rendered into all languages, into verse and prose, into songs and pictures, and cut up into proverbs; so that the occasion which gave the saint's meaning the form of a conversation, or of a prayer, or of a code of laws, is immaterial, compared with the universality of its application. So it fares with the wise Shakspeare and his book of life. He wrote the airs for all our modern music: he wrote the text of modern life; the text of manners: he drew the man of England and Europe; the father of the man in America: he drew the man, and described the day, and what is done in it: he read the hearts of men and women, their probity, and their second thought, and wiles; the wiles of innocence, and the transitions by which virtues and vices slide into their contraries: he could divide the mother's part from the father's part in the face of the child, or draw the fine demarcations of freedom and of fate: he knew the laws of repression which make the police of nature: and all the sweets and all the terrors of human lot lay in his mind as truly but as softly as the landscape lies on the eye. And the importance of this wisdom of life sinks the form, as of Drama or Epic, out of notice. 'Tis like making a question concerning the paper on which a king's message is written.

"He wrote the text of modern life" is the heart of this matter: Shakespeare invented us, and continues to contain us. We are now in an era of so-called "cultural criticism," which devalues all imaginative literature, and which particularly demotes and debases Shakespeare. Politicizing literary study has destroyed literary study, and may yet destroy learning itself. Shakespeare has influenced the world far more than it initially influenced Shakespeare. The com-

mon assumption of all the Resenters is that state power is
everything and individual subjectivity is nothing, even if
that subjectivity belonged to William Shakespeare. Fright-
ened by their irrational social order, the English Renais-
sance playwrights, in this account, either became time-
servers or subverters or a mixture of both, while being
caught in the irony that even their textual subversions
helped to enhance state power, a power rather surprisingly
held to be reliant upon theatricality. I return to Emerson
for an antidote to all this power-mongering. Who wrote
the text of modern life, Shakespeare or the Elizabethan-
Jacobean political establishment? Who invented the human,
as we know it, Shakespeare or the court and its ministers?
Who influenced Shakespeare's actual text more, William
Cecil, Lord Burghley, the First Secretary to Her Majesty, or
Christopher Marlowe? What we once used to call "imaginative
literature" is indistinguishable from literary influence, and has
only an inessential relationship to state power. If any stan-
dards of judgment at all are to survive our current cultural
reductiveness, then we need to reassert that high literature
is exactly that, an aesthetic achievement, and not state
propaganda, even if literature can be used, has been used,
and doubtless will be used to serve the interests of a state,
or of a social class, or of a religion, or of men against
women, whites against blacks, Westerners against Eastern-
ers. I know of no more dismal contemporary comedy, either
in Great Britain or the United States, than the revolution-
ary pretenses of our academics, who persuade themselves
that they speak for the insulted and injured of the world by
denying the aesthetic primacy of Shakespeare, or by insist-
ing that aesthetic eminence of any sort is merely a capitalis-
tic mystification. Our Trinculos and Stephanos have arrived,
they say, to free Caliban from bondage to Prospero. Here
also Shakespeare has anticipated them, and teaches us that
what the Resenters truly resent is not state power but

Shakespeare's power, the power of invention. Unable to be Nietzsche, who has made them all belated, our Resenters do not wish merely to re-proclaim the Death of God, so they turn instead to proclaiming what only can be called the Death of Shakespeare.

Coleridge spoke of the ever-living men and women, the canonical writers, a most archaic way of speaking in this present age, when students are taught to scorn the Dead White European Males, or again, most simply William Shakespeare. The largest truth of literary influence is that it is an irresistible anxiety: Shakespeare will not allow you to bury him, or escape him, or replace him. We have, almost all of us, thoroughly internalized the power of Shakespeare's plays, frequently without having attended them or read them. When the German poet Stefan George called *The Divine Comedy* "the Book and School of the Ages," he was speaking only about the education of great poets. All the rest of us inescapably learn that Shakespeare's plays constitute the Book and School of the Ages. I am not speaking as an essentialist humanist, which I do not pretend to be, or as a theorist of criticism, which is also not my role. As a theorist of poetic influence, I am an anxious partaker of Shakespeare, the inevitable role for all of us, who belatedly follow after Shakespeare's creation of our minds and spirits. Literature, that is to say Shakespeare, cannot be thought of in terms only of knowledge, as if all his metaphors pertained only to knowing. Shakespeare's pervasive terms are metaphors of willing, and so they enter the domain of the lie. Most of our understandings of the will are Will's, as it were, because Shakespeare invented the domain of those metaphors of willing that Freud named the drives of Love and Death.

Our true relation to Shakespeare is that it is vain to historicize or politicize him, because we are monumentally over-influenced by him. No strong writer since Shakespeare can avoid his influence, again excluding the recalcitrant French, who probably will not accept even the shrunken or pygmy dramatist I have called "French Shakespeare." Frank Kermode speaks of "the fantastic range of possibilities" that are explored by Shakespeare's tragedies, and that seems to me precisely right. Who can defend herself or himself, if that self has any literary possibilities whatsoever, from what truly is a fantastic range of possibilities, larger than any single one of us can hope to apprehend. Resenters of canonical literature are nothing more or less than deniers of Shakespeare. They are not social revolutionaries or even cultural rebels. They are sufferers of the anxieties of Shakespeare's influence.

II

Oscar Wilde sublimely remarked that "all bad poetry is sincere." Doubtless it would be wrong to say that all great poetry is insincere, but of course almost all of it necessarily tells lies, fictions essential to literary art. Authentic, high literature relies upon troping, a turning away not only from the literal but from prior tropes. Like criticism, which is either part of literature or nothing at all, great writing is always at work strongly (or weakly) misreading previous writing. Any stance that anyone takes up towards a metaphorical work will itself be metaphorical. My useful (for me) decades-long critical quarrel with Paul de Man, a radiant intelligence, finally centered upon just the contention stated in the previous sentence. He insisted that an epistemological stance in regard to a literary work was the only way out of the tropological labyrinth, while I replied that such a stance was no more or less a trope than any other. Irony, in its prime sense of allegory, saying one thing while suggesting another, is the epistemological trope-of-tropes, and for de Man constituted the condition of literary language itself, producing that "permanent parabasis of meaning" studied by deconstructionists.

When is Shakespeare sincere? That absurd question returns us to the curious fiction that Shakespeare and nature are everywhere the same. I myself was a victim of that fiction when I denied, in this book, that Shakespeare ever experienced any anxiety of influence in regard to his prime precursor and rival Ovidian, Christopher Marlowe, only two months or so older than Shakespeare but the dominant London playwright from 1587 until his violent death in 1593, aged twenty-nine. In 1587, Shakespeare went up from Stratford to London, and perhaps began as a printer's apprentice. This may have given him an aversion for proof-reading (having held such a job, in my early youth, I have been a dreadful reader of my own proofs in consequence). Certainly Shakespeare seems never to have read proof even for "authorized" quartos, except for *Venus and Adonis* and *The Rape of Lucrece*, both dedicated to his patron (some think also his lover), the Earl of Southhampton. After being a printer's devil, Shakespeare may have begun in the theater as a prompter's assistant, and went on to become an actor before writing for the stage. Marlowe, though like Shakespeare the son of an artisan, had a university education and doubtless would have scorned acting, a socially ambiguous profession at that time.

Ben Jonson, the other great playwright of the era of Marlowe and Shakespeare, abandoned acting after he became established, but Shakespeare certainly did not, though we have only limited information as to his actor's career. Neither a clown, nor a hero, nor a villain in his roles, Shakespeare seems to have been respected as what we now, rather oddly, call a "character actor." We know that he played the Ghost in *Hamlet*, and old Adam in *As You Like It*, and several kings, and we can suspect that he acted the Player-King in *Hamlet*, a natural doubling. Shakespeare perhaps gave up acting when he was forty, about the time that he composed *Measure For Measure* and *Othello*. Meredith Anne Skura's remarkable *Shakespeare the Actor and the Purposes of Playing* (1993) centers upon the plays' awareness of the pride and degradation of being an actor, an overt, narcissistic ambivalence that may not have been entirely Shakespeare's own but that appears crucial to his art. Christopher Marlowe certainly was crucial to Shakespeare's art from the early tetralogy of the three parts of *Henry VI* and *Richard III* (1589–93) through *Titus Andronicus* (1594) until Shakespeare surmounted Marlowe's *Edward II* in *Richard II* (1595), two years after Marlowe was murdered in a tavern brawl, probably by orders of the government, whom Marlowe had served as what we now call an intelligence agent.

It is hardly possible that Marlowe and Shakespeare did not know one another personally, since they shared four years of rivalry in writing for the London stage. Shakespeare, much more impressive in his early comedies than in his first histories or his first tragedy, emerged into an aesthetic realm sublimely beyond Marlowe's when he began to fashion the great roles that owe nothing to Marlowe's superb caricatures, such as Tamburlaine, and Barabas, hero-villain of *The Jew of Malta*. Richard III, and Aaron the Moor in *Titus Andronicus*, are altogether Marlovian. Richard II is somewhere in between Marlowe's Edward II and Hamlet; but Juliet and Mercutio, Bottom and Puck, Shylock and Falstaff began to make Marlowe seem rudimentary. Compared to mature Shakespeare, Marlowe is still an extraordinary poet, yet no dramatist at all. But to say, as I did in this book, that Shakespeare swallowed up Marlowe the way a whale scoops up a minnow was to ignore the extraordinary case of indigestion that Marlowe caused the Moby-Dick of all playwrights. Marlowe never developed, and never would have, even had he seen thirty. Shakespeare was an extravagant developer, experimenting down to the end. The Bible and Chaucer taught Shakespeare some of his secrets in representing human beings, while Marlowe had little interest in what Dr. Johnson was to call "just representations of general nature." And yet Marlowe haunted Shakespeare, who defensively parodied his forerunner while resolving that the author of *The Jew of Malta* would become for him primarily the way *not* to go, whether in life or in art. He must have known, though, that Marlowe had emancipated the theater from overt moralities and moralizings, and opened the way to pleasing enormous audiences, who were not trying to become better or wiser through attending a play. Russell Fraser, in his *Young Shakespeare* (1988), rightly says that, with Marlowe, "Shakespeare's story begins," and adds that Shakespeare's *King John* is too wounded by Marlowe to be a success, which may be true. *Titus Andronicus* I can read only as a deliberate send-up both of Marlowe's friend, Thomas Kyd, and of Marlowe himself, but most Shakespeare scholars argue otherwise. Yet what is Aaron the Moor if not a monstrous blow-up of Marlowe's Barabas? Even Shylock, despite Shakespeare's equivocal anti-Semitism, is a reaction-formation to Marlowe's cartoonish Jew of Malta, who hardly could say "If you prick us, do we not bleed?," just as Shylock would not cry out "sometimes I go about and poison wells."

I never meant by "the anxiety of influence" a Freudian Oedipal rivalry, despite a rhetorical flourish or two in this book. A Shakespearean reading of Freud, which I favor over a Freudian reading of Shakespeare or anyone else, reveals that Freud suffered from a Hamlet complex (the true name of the Oedipus Complex) or an anxiety of influence in regard to Shakespeare. Since I have argued this matter at some length in a recent book (*The Western Canon*, 1994), I need say little about it here, except to murmur again how weakly misread *The Anxiety of Influence* has been, and continues to be. Any adequate reader of this book, which means anyone of some literary sensibility who is not a commissar or an ideologue, Left *or* Right, will see that influence-anxiety does not so much concern the forerunner but rather is an anxiety achieved in and by the story, novel, play, poem, or essay. The anxiety may or may not be internalized by the later writer, depending upon temperament and circumstances, yet that hardly matters: the strong poem is the achieved anxiety. "Influence" is a metaphor, one that implicates a matrix of relationships—imagistic, temporal, spiritual, psychological—all of them ultimately defensive in their nature. What matters most (and it is the central point of this book) is that the anxiety of influence *comes out of* a complex act of strong misreading, a creative interpretation that I call "poetic misprision." What writers may experience as anxiety, and what their works are compelled to manifest, are the *consequence* of poetic misprision, rather than the *cause* of it. The strong misreading comes first; there must be a profound act of reading that is a kind of falling in love with a literary work. That reading is likely to be idiosyncratic, and it is almost certain to be ambivalent, though the ambivalence may be veiled. Without Keats's reading of Shakespeare, Milton, and Wordsworth, we could not have Keats's odes and sonnets and his two *Hyperions*. Without Tennyson's reading of Keats, we would have almost no Tennyson. Wallace Stevens, hostile to all suggestions that he owed anything to his reading of precursor poets, would have left us nothing of value but for Walt Whitman, whom Stevens sometimes scorned, almost never overtly imitated, yet uncannily resurrected:

> Sigh for me, night-wind, in the noisy leaves of the oak.
> I am tired. Sleep for me, heaven over the hill.
> Shout for me, loudly and loudly, joyful sun, when you rise.

III

In ways that need not be doctrinal, strong poems are always omens of resurrection. The dead may or may not return, but their voice comes alive, paradoxically never by mere imitation, but in the agonistic misprision performed upon powerful forerunners by only the most gifted of their successors. Ibsen loathed influence more perhaps than anyone else, particularly since his authentic forerunner was Shakespeare, much more than Goethe. This horror of contamination by Shakespeare fortunately found its best Ibsenite expression in the multiple ways the Norse playwright discovered for evading Shakespeare. Mrs. Alving in *Ghosts* seems at first to have nothing Shakespearean about her, but her extraordinary capacity for willing changes in herself is nothing if not Shakespearean, relying as it does upon a Shakespearean and very subtle mode of foregrounding. Hedda Gabler, as much as Dostoevsky's Svidrigailov and Stavrogin, finds her ancestors in those pioneer nihilists, Iago and the Edmund of *King Lear*. Still intoxicated by the High Romantic poets when I wrote *The Anxiety of Influence*, I tried to confine the phenomenon of creative misprision to post-Enlightenment writers, a false emphasis that I corrected in *A Map of Misreading* and subsequent books. The irony of one era cannot be the irony of another, but influence-anxieties are embedded in the agonistic basis of all imaginative literature. Agon or the contest for aesthetic supremacy was very overt in ancient Greek literature, but this has been a difference of degree rather than of kind between different cultures. Plato's contest with Homer is the central agon of Western literature, but there are many rival struggles, down to the parodistic matches between Hemingway and his precursors, and the followers of Hemingway with the master.

Cultural belatedness is never acceptable to a major writer, though Borges made a career out of exploiting his secondariness. Belatedness seems to me not a historical condition at all, but one that belongs to the literary situation as such. Resentful historicists of several persuasions—stemming from Marx, Foucault, and political feminism—now study literature essentially as peripheral social history. What has been discarded is the reader's solitude, a subjectivity that has been rejected because it supposedly possesses "no social being." Tony Kushner, the dramatist of *Angels in America*, generously assigns his authorship to many others, a curious literalization on his part of Brecht's plagiaristic stance. Peculiar as this may be, it is clarity itself compared to the "French Shakespeare" that now dominates the ruined shards of the Anglo-American academic world. Shakespeare's solitude has vanished, and has been replaced by a playwright whose work is supposed to overthrow the power-systems of the Renaissance world, whether based on class or gender. This peculiar, rather desperate view of Shakespeare purports to be revolutionary but pragmatically amounts to substituting highly selective contexts for the actual Shakespearean text. We know nothing authentic about Shakespeare's politics, or his religion, or his social outlook, and heaping up extraneous contexts has served mostly to enhance the resentments of the already resentful. Our belatedness evidently exceeds Shakespeare's by more than the burden of our four centuries of additional history.

An awareness of the anxiety of influence—our own, in regard to Shakespeare—might partly cleanse us of the resentments of a scholarly belatedness. Historicizing, politicizing, even feminizing Shakespeare—all are redundant operations: Shakespeare always was there before us. He emancipated no one (that we know of) from the power-structures of his own day, and cannot liberate us from any societal enclosures in our current squalor. If you quarry Shakespeare for ultimates, you emerge with nothing, and you are in danger of pragmatically equating him with his own superb nihilists. What are his energies? Was his relation to Marlowe, beyond that of aesthetic rivalry, somehow part of the social energies of their shared era? I would venture that, far more than any other writer since the pre-Socratic sages, Shakespeare's energies so fuse rhetoric, psychology, and cosmology that we cannot distinguish them from one another in his greatest plays. They are one entity for him, as they were for Empedocles and the Sophists who followed Empedocles. A purely rhetorical criticism, a psychological reductiveness, a cosmological perspective—none of these alone can hope to comprehend Shakespeare, or any other writer who begins to approach his eminence. More than any other purely secular author, Shakespeare makes history far more than history makes Shakespeare. Returning Shakespeare to history is a disheartened endeavour, and to a considerable degree an ahistorical adventure. What is literary history, or social history for that matter? Perspectivism, with all its entrapments, dominates "history," as Nietzsche eloquently indicated in his essay on the use and abuse of history for life, one of my starting points for what became *The Anxiety of Influence*.

Emerson, who chose his essay "History" to lead off *Essays: First Series*, memorably advised us that biography is always the prior mode:

> We are always coming up with the emphatic facts of history in our private experience, and verifying them here. All history becomes subjective; in other words, there is properly no history; only biography. Every mind must know the whole lesson for itself,—must go over the whole ground. What it does not see, what it does not live, it will not know. What the former age has epitomized into a formula or rule for manipular con-

venience, it will lose all the good of verifying for itself, by means of the wall of that rule. Somewhere, sometime, it will demand and find compensation for that loss by doing the work itself.

Biographical criticism, long out of fashion, scarcely works for Shakespeare, about whom we know only externals, except for the *Sonnets*, where we never can be certain what is formal and what is not. But a good biography of Shakespeare, like Russell Fraser's, is preferable to any historicism, because at least we are alone with Shakespeare and Fraser, rather than being propagandized by an academic sect or coven. Even better is the only good novel written about Shakespeare, Anthony Burgess's Joycean *Nothing Like the Sun*, where we are returned to the library scene in *Ulysses*, with its fecund speculations about Shakespeare's relation to Hamlet. Joyce, Burgess, and Fraser in their different ways acknowledge the contingency that Shakespeare imposes upon us, which is that we are so influenced by him that we cannot get outside of him. Criticism necessarily fails when it deludes itself into the smugness of not seeing that we remain enclosed by Shakespeare. The only instruments by which we can examine him were either invented or perfected by Shakespeare himself. Wittgenstein, who disliked Shakespeare, tried to defend philosophy from the best mind we can know by insisting that Shakespeare was less a writer than he was "a creator of language." It would be nearer the truth to say that Falstaff, Hamlet, and Iago are creators of language, while Shakespeare, by their means, created *us*. Language, despite Heidegger and his French flock, does not do the thinking for Shakespeare, who more than any other writer, or any other person that we know of, thought everything through again for himself. Shakespeare did not think one thought and one thought only; rather scandalously, he thought all thoughts, for all of us. A new Bardolatry is not the issue, nor is hyperbole possible when we seek to estimate Shakespeare's influence during the four centuries since his death. Doubtless Shakespeare, at heart always a player, conceived every part he ever wrote as a role for a specific actor, but it is an evasion now to regard them as roles only, since they have become roles *for us*, whether we are players or not. When we are born, we cry that we are come unto this great stage of fools. Lear echoes the Wisdom of Solomon, but the Scriptural authority for the pronouncement is Shakespeare's and not the Bible's. We are fools of time bound for the undiscovered country, more than we are children of God returning to heaven. The issue is not belief but our human nature, so intensified by Shakespeare as to be his re-invention. How can we historicize Shakespeare if we are children of Shakespeare, mapping our origins and our horizons in his diction, in his astonishing vocabulary of some 22,000 separate words?

IV

To say that Shakespeare and poetic influence are nearly identical is not very different from observing that Shakespeare is the western literary canon. Some would argue that "aesthetic value" is an invention of Kant's, but pragmatically it is the aesthetic supremacy of Shakespeare that overdetermines our judgment of literary value. In Hazlitt's superb essay, "On Poetry in General," there are about twenty citations of Shakespeare, but even Hazlitt may not have been aware of how Shakespearean his cognition had become:

> We see the thing ourselves, and show it to others as we feel it to exist, and as, in spite of ourselves, we are compelled to think of it. The imagination, by thus embodying and turning them to shape, gives an obvious relief to the indistinct and impor-

tunate cravings of the will.—We do not wish the thing to be so; but we wish it to appear such as it is. For knowledge is conscious power; and the mind is no longer, in this case, the dupe, though it may be the victim of vice or folly.

"On Poetry in General" twice quotes from *Macbeth*, yet *Macbeth* in particular certainly is not Hazlitt's subject in the essay. Still, this passage concerns not imagination in general, but Macbeth's dangerously proleptic imagination, which is hallucinatory and which dominates Macbeth's consciousness. Hazlitt is purging himself of Macbeth's will, by means of Shakespeare's art, which both contaminates and cures Hazlitt. After Dr. Johnson, there is no finer critic in the language than Hazlitt, who nevertheless yields to Shakespeare's influence without knowing that he has yielded.

The judgment, even the taste, of Shakespeare's contemporary audiences scarcely differs from our own. Hamlet and Falstaff were Shakespeare's greatest successes then, as they are now. Ben Jonson and nearly every other dramatist of the period from 1590 through 1630 complained bitterly about their audiences, but we have no complaints from Shakespeare about his reception, as opposed to how his actors performed him. All of our evidence suggests that Shakespeare's influence began almost immediately and has prevailed these four centuries since he died. If there ever has been a universal literary art, that art is Shakespeare's, an art that seemed nature to his contemporaries, and that has become nature for us. If there is any mystery to Shakespeare, it is in his large usurpation of "nature" and of all literary art before him that, to him, seemed useful for his purposes. Ovid, Chaucer, and Marlowe fused into Shakespeare's composite precursor, as his contemporaries evidently understood. They seem to have understood also that Shakespeare established a new norm for representation.

"Distinct," as a noun meaning a separate person or thing, is very rare, and may have been invented by Shakespeare for his elegy, "The Phoenix and Turtle":

> So they loved as love in twain
> Had the essence but in one,
> Two distincts, division none:
> Number there in love was slain.

Dryden, in the Preface to his "corrected" version of *Troilus and Cressida* (1679), says that Shakespeare must be allowed "to have made his characters distinct," an accurate acknowledgment taken up by Dr. Johnson in his Preface to his edition of Shakespeare (1765). Johnson improves upon Dryden: "Characters thus ample and general were not easily discriminated and preserved, yet perhaps no poet ever kept his personages more distinct from each other." "Distinct" is the center of praise here, and marks Shakespeare's endless power of influencing all representation since. No one before or since has had so acute an ear, inner and outer, and has so varied the voices of his characters, rendering them so consistently distinct. Once again we confront the strength of Shakespeare's usurpations, both of nature and of art. The anxiety of influence, as a critical idea, can confront no more severe test than Shakespeare's total freedom of representation, once he had revised the Marlovian hero-villain into something light years beyond Marlowe's interests and aspirations. I return to Shakespeare's agon with Marlowe in order to see what illumination Shakespeare's triumph can bring both to our understanding of his "distinct" characterization and of the process of poetic influence itself.

Marlowe is so far from representing either human character or human personality that he becomes grotesque when read against mature Shakespeare. Like the Edmund of *King Lear*, whom I take as Shakespeare's Last Judgment upon Marlowe, neither Marlowe nor his protagonists manifest anything we can recognize as human affect. As a poet, Marlowe is closer to Rimbaud and Hart Crane than he is to Shakespeare. Rhetoricity or word-consciousness replaces self-consciousness, and the normal mode becomes invocation or incantation. The true surprise of Marlowe's influence upon Shakespeare is that it lasted as long as it did; it is still there in *King John* (1594, at the latest), but it wanes when the Bastard Faulconbridge concludes his lament for John, and we pass to the world of *Richard II* (1595). For some six years, after he composed the First Part of *Henry VI*, Shakespeare had been creatively obsessed with Marlowe, and that seems to me the most improbable reality that we ever encounter in Shakespeare. What was it that fascinated him, in his relationship to the unlikeliest precursor he could have been found by, and what misprision of Marlowe kept Marlowe alive in Shakespeare for so long? Marlowe's overwhelming importance as the great formal innovator in Elizabethan drama is not in question. His "mighty line," the "brave sublunary things" of his exalted rhetoric, and his emancipation of the theater from its theological moral heritage were all bound to influence Shakespeare, just as they influenced even Ben Jonson. But Jonson was not haunted by Marlowe; Shakespeare was, for at least six years, and then paid a final tribute to Marlowe in *As You Like It* (1599), the least Marlovian of all possible plays, composed six years after Marlowe's murder. I have suggested already that in *King Lear* (1605), Shakespeare takes a sly, final backward glance at Marlowe in Edmund, the most sophisticated and coldest of all Shakespearean villains. Long after Marlowe was exorcised, Shakespeare retained the prime resource of the hero-villain, who had been crudely Marlovian in *Richard III*, but is totally non-Marlovian in *Macbeth*. Doubtless the Bible, Ovid, and Chaucer were deeper and more fecund influences upon

Shakespeare, the master of characterization, but only Marlowe inspired in him both ambivalence and anxiety. It is impossible that Shakespeare and Marlowe did not know one another personally, particularly from 1590 to May 1593 (when Marlowe was killed), years in which *Tamburlaine*, *The Jew of Malta*, and *Edward II* were being played in London against *Henry VI*, *Titus Andronicus*, and *Richard III*, all of them Marlovian works. We have no anecdotes connecting the two, so presumably they were not close friends, as Shakespeare and Jonson were, or even good acquaintances, as Shakespeare and George Chapman probably were. But Marlowe's literary circle—Chapman, Kyd, Nashe—were all known to Shakespeare; there were no more than two dozen playwrights supplying the acting companies during the early 1590s. Anthony Burgess, in his posthumously published *A Dead Man in Deptford*, his attempt to do for Marlowe what he had done for a fictionalized Shakespeare in *Nothing Like the Sun*, unfortunately creates only one conversation between Shakespeare and Marlowe, concerning their rather unlikely joint labor upon *Henry VI, Part One*. Adding to that creation is beyond me, but I want to use our intertextual evidence to get as close to the poetic version of such a conversation as I can. Marlowe is an aggressive dramatist, but not a subtle one. His "atheism" or "Epicureanism," as defined by his contemporaries, is expressed by Tamburlaine and Barabas, in ways that we find equivocal, whether as faith or as disbelief. But Marlowe's sheer drive is unmistakable; the first part of *Tamburlaine* and *The Jew of Malta* move with a remorseless energy, very difficult for an audience (or an aspiring dramatist) to resist. Shakespeare in time learned how to form a play with an even fiercer drive; more than *Doctor Faustus*, *Macbeth* is an economical shot out of hell. We do not associate Shakespeare with any particular rhetorical trope, unlike Marlowe, who is synonomous with hyperbole. Shakespeare ironizes and qualifies his overreachers, while his own, uncanny mastery of language, his extraordinary, Mozartean facility of composition, makes it unlikely that he was enthralled by Marlowe's language alone. There are signs of acute ambivalence even in Shakespeare's earliest Marlovianism, but something in Marlowe would not let Shakespeare go before 1593, at the earliest.

The speeches of Marlowe's protagonists move with such rapidity that we feel they (and Marlowe) are in a great hurry, not necessarily to get anywhere, but to dominate us through the power of their rhetoric. This is what the Australian poet A. D. Hope has called, following Tamburlaine, "the argument of arms," which holds that the struggle for supreme power is central both to poetry and to warfare. Marlowe's hyperboles fuse the pen and the sword, in a union less phallic than we are likely, in our era, to suppose. Phantasmagorias of power, Marlowe's staple, have very little to do with sexual possession, but catalog instead the infinite inventory of an endless will, a more-than-imperial will. Such an inventory piles up all manner of delights, in a mode of enticement imitated by Jonson's Volpone and Sir Epicure Mammon, but all the commodities thus heaped together, women included, are there as trophies of domination. The rhetorical drive, in Marlowe, is identical with the aggressivity of warfare, yet that seems an understatement in regard to the most hyperbolical of poet-dramatists. Again, that makes him an enemy-brother, an Edmund to Shakespeare's Edgar. If we are to account for Marlowe having stayed so long in Shakespeare's work, we can find it only in the realm of the antithetical.

Marlowe was the star of the "University Wits" (Lyly, Peele, Greene, Lodge, Nashe), who were socially superior to the actor-playwrights Shakespeare and Jonson. If we add to this Marlowe's priority over Shakespeare, in every genre except comedy, then Marlowe very likely would have been a stimulating burden for the apprentice Shakespeare. And despite a peculiar tendency of modern scholars to Christianize Marlowe's plays, Shakespeare must have heard in them their curious "natural religion" (to call it that) which is not easily reconciled with Protestant Christianity. Tamburlaine, the scourge of God, performs his office on behalf of a semi-Moloch who appears to relish vast burned offerings of entire cities and their populations. It would be absurd, on the basis of Shakespeare's thirty-eight plays, to announce their dramatist's religious stance, whether pious, skeptical, or nihilistic. But Shakespeare seems to have a clear idea of Marlowe's religion when his portrait of Marlowe, the Edmund of *King Lear*, invokes Nature as his goddess, and urges the gods to stand up for bastards. Edmund's power over his dupes—Edgar and Gloucester in one mode, Regan and Goneril in the other—is a recall of Tamburlaine's extraordinary power of "pathetical persuasion," not only over his supporters and his enemies, and his beloved Zenocrate, but over Marlowe's large and enthralled audiences. Shakespeare doubtless had watched Marlowe played, and wondered at the wholly new phenomenon of two to three thousand spectators emotionally captured by the actor Alleyn's bombastic declamation of Marlowe's hyperboles. Something unexpected had entered English stage history, and Shakespeare must have understood that Marlowe's and Kyd's speaking cartoons were first steps towards a different kind of playing. Origins are of peculiar importance for strong writers. No great poet ever has journeyed as far from his origins as Shakespeare did, and there are no more backward glances at Marlowe after Edgar slays Edmund (shall we read that as the irony of Shakespeare finally ending Marlowe?), and we pass on to the final tragedies and the romances.

Marlowe, for Shakespeare, was primarily a personal image of the dramatist's power over the audience, a power only uneasily allied to traditional morality, societal constraints, or orthodox pieties. Freedom, the poet-playwright's freedom from what for Marlowe were irrelevant expectations, was his precursor's largest legacy to Shakespeare. Marlowe's freedom was expressed by his personality perhaps as much as by the language of his plays, with catastrophic consequences. Shakespeare, on the surface one of the least colorful of personalities, conveyed his freedom much more subtly, not only in the language of his plays but in their thinking, and in their characters' thoughts and emotions. There remains the stubborn problem of how much Shakespeare was in control of his memories of Marlowe's language. After *Henry VI*, an ironic inflection almost invariably conditions the Marlovian recalls, and yet many of these are less allusive than they are something else, repetitions perhaps, usually in a finer tone. The fascination with Marlowe remained; one could almost term it a seduction by Marlowe. Shakespeare's freedom manifested itself multivalently, producing the profoundly complex triumphs of Falstaff, Hamlet, and Iago, each a cosmos exposing Tamburlaine, Faustus, and Barabas as caricatures. But what larger provocation did Shakespeare have for his invention of the human than Marlowe's emotional power as a mere cartoonist? Talbot in Shakespeare's *Henry VI* is only a cartoon, as are Aaron the Moor and Richard III, but as caricatures they carried on Marlowe's kind of success. Monsters and puppets, given high, presumptive language, were sufficient to move audiences about as much as Marlowe had moved them. Shakespeare desired not only to move them still more, but to take them into the interior with him. The growing inner self, our incessant predicament, is more a Shakespearean than a Lutheran or Calvinist invention. Montaigne shares with Shakespeare the prestige of explorer here, and perhaps contributed to Hamlet's self through the medium of John Florio's manuscript of his ongoing translation. I return to Shakespeare's patience with his audience in contrast to his impatience with his actors. Shakespeare's audience had first been Marlowe's and, to a lesser extent, Kyd's. They had prompted Shakespeare, and as he seems to have understood, they had prepared Shakespeare's audience for him. The freedom of the poet-dramatist to some degree had to be granted by his audience.

Sir Francis Bacon, considering "the action of the theatre," brilliantly tells us: "Certain it is, though a great secret in nature, that the minds of men in company are more open to affections and impressions than when alone." Shakespeare exploits this realization throughout his work, and doubtless reflected on how different, and how similar, an audience is to a congregation, an army, or a crowd addressed by a politician. The school where that reflection began almost certainly, as I have said, was a Marlovian audience, and so the first lesson would have emphasized the power of the auditory. *A Midsummer Night's Dream*, with its highly un-Marlovian Bottom, has little of Marlowe in it except for Shakespeare's extraordinary mastery in having the auditory dimension dominate over the visual, in what, as much as *The Tempest*, is a visionary play. But *The Tempest*, like *The Winter's Tale*, plays as much upon what the audience sees or doesn't quite see as upon what they hear. We are so far away from Marlowe in the later Shakespeare that we can be tempted to forget the master's lesson that the poet's freedom depends upon an auditory engulfment of the playgoers. Shakespeare does not forget, and except for certain uncanny moments, his internalization of the Marlovian music is incessant. We are back at the origin again, with the audiences that Tamburlaine seduced, while Shakespeare listened and saw, and analyzed the elements of the seduction, which worked upon literate and illiterate alike. There, I assume, is another clue as to why Marlowe was so difficult for Shakespeare to exorcise. Brave, vaunting passages had a tendency to sound Marlovian even when they were not at all like Marlowe, in style or rhythm or texture. Poetry, or the poetic, discoursing of itself upon a stage, had been usurped by Marlowe, and this was a very formidable usurpation to overturn. Shakespeare had not quite managed it even with *Julius Caesar* or with *Richard II*. When Hotspur declaims in *Henry IV, Part One*, Shakespeare takes care that we should note the muted ghost of Marlowe, a ghost driven out in the agonistic interchanges between Hal and Falstaff, ungrateful student and love-smitten teacher. When Hamlet begins to speak, Marlowe is not even a shade, and has ceased to trouble the heir who transcended him. But that is certainly a long day's dying, and the coda of the Marlovian Edmund testifies to Marlowe's lingering into the Shakespearean twilight.

Shakespeare may have appreciated the irony that Marlowe had alerted him to the psychology of dominating an audience by the agency of eloquent cartoons who themselves were psychologically void. The greater irony is that Shakespeare's path away from Marlowe was one of progressive internalization, culminating in the hallucinatory imagination of Macbeth. This internalization begins very ineptly in *Richard III*, where Shakespeare mars his drama by mawkishly attempting to impart some pathos to the tyrant on the eve of his death. But I will consider that engrossing, bad, and revealing soliloquy of Richard III only after a glance at Shakespeare's first plays.

Henry VI, in all its three parts, has few admirers, and today scarcely sounds to us like Shakespeare. Only Jack Cade's rebellion, in the Second Part, has a touch of life, an oasis amidst a desert of sub-Marlovian rhetoric. This is Shakespeare's starting point, and *Tamburlaine* and *The Jew of Malta* seem always in his ear, except when he escapes to what is already his own prose: "the first thing we do, let's kill all the lawyers." Yet the plays did very well, a puzzle to us now primarily because almost all the characters speak with Marlowe's voice. When the future Richard III emerges in his full horror at the close of the Third Part, we still can only barely distinguish his tones, as opposed to his sentiments, from anyone else's.

Richard III, like the *Tamburlaine* plays, has lost much of its popularity, partly because it is too formal and stylized, rather too rigidly Marlovian in its impact. Shakespeare vainly attempts to break out of that rigidity, when Richard wakes up out of a nightmare, just before going out to his defeat and death at Bosworth Field. Without warning, we are plunged into the abyss of Richard's precarious internalization, as Shakespeare attempts to alter the tyrant from a Marlovian cartoon to a psychological portrait:

> The lights burn blue. It is now dead midnight.
> Cold fearful drops stand on my trembling flesh.
> What do I fear? Myself? There's none else by.
> Richard loves Richard, that is, I [am] I.
> Is there a murtherer here? No. Yes, I am.
> Then fly. What, from myself? Great reason why—
> Lest I revenge. What, myself upon myself?
> Alack, I love myself. Wherefore? For any good
> That I myself have done unto myself?
> O no! Alas, I rather hate myself
> For hateful deeds committed by myself.
> I am a villain; yet I lie, I am not.
> Fool, of thyself speak well; fool, do not flatter:
> My conscience hath a thousand several tongues,
> And every tongue brings in a several tale,
> And every tale condemns me for a villain.
> Perjury, perjury, in the highest degree;
> Murther, stern murther, in the direst degree;
> All several sins, all us'd in each degree,
> Throng to the bar, crying all, "Guilty! guilty!"
> I shall despair; there is no creature loves me,
> And if I die no soul will pity me.

And wherefore should they, since that I myself
Find in myself no pity to myself?
Methought the souls of all that I had murther'd
Came to my tent, and every one did threat
To-morrow's vengeance on the head of Richard.

It is not only the poorest writing in the play, but perhaps
the weakest passage in all Shakespeare. We cannot accom-
modate it, since there has not been the slightest sign of
an inner self in Richard before this disjointed soliloquy.
Having nearly completed another Marlovian drama, to
complement the *Henry VI* plays, Shakespeare rebelled, but
failed. He had as yet no sure procedure for invoking
inwardness, and his misprision of Marlowe here seems
to confuse the cartoon character with the psychologically
responsive audience, as though he would emulate his pre-
cursor but then go beyond him by dragging the audience
onto the stage. This agon with Marlowe is much more suc-
cessful in Aaron the Moor than in Richard III, but then
Aaron is the one ornament of *Titus Andronicus.*

That savage play, perhaps revised by Shakespeare from
an earlier version by George Peele, is an unwholesome
blend of an authentic tragedy-of-blood and what must be
a kind of send-up, a parodistic burlesque of Marlowe and
Kyd, with Aaron the Moor as a demonic answer to Barabas,
Jew of Malta. Deliberately alluding to the most outrageous
speech of Barabas, Shakespeare attempts to out-Marlowe
Marlowe:

BARABAS: As for myself, I walk abroad a-nights,
And kill sick people groaning under walls.
Sometimes I go about and poison wells;
And now and then, to cherish Christian thieves,
I am content to lose some of my crowns,
That I may, walking in my gallery,
See 'em go pinion'd along by my door.
Being young, I studied physic, and began

To practise first upon the Italian;
There I enrich'd the priests with burials,
And always kept the sexton's arms in use
With digging graves and ringing dead men's knells.
And, after that, was I an engineer,
And in the wars 'twixt France and Germany,
Under the pretence of helping Charles the Fifth,
Slew friend and enemy with my stratagems:
Then after that was I an usurer,
And with extorting, cozening, forfeiting,
And tricks belonging unto brokery,
I fill'd the gaols with bankrupts in a year,
And with young orphans planted hospitals;
And every moon made some or other mad,
And now and then one hang himself for grief,
Pinning upon his breast a long great scroll
How I with interest tormented him.
But mark how I am blest for plaguing them:
I have as much coin as will buy the town.
But tell me now, how hast thou spent thy time?

AARON: Ay, that I had not done a thousand more.
Even now I curse the day—and yet I think
Few come within the compass of my curse—
Wherein I did not some notorious ill:
As kill a man, or else devise his death,
Ravish a maid, or plot the way to do it,
Accuse some innocent, and forswear myself,
Set deadly enmity between two friends,
Make poor men's cattle break their necks,
Set fire on barns and haystalks in the night,
And bid the owners quench them with their tears.
Oft have I digg'd up dead men from their graves,
And set them upright at their dear friends' door,
Even when their sorrows almost was forgot,
And on their skins, as on the bark of trees,
Have with my knife carved in Roman letters,
"Let not your sorrow die, though I am dead."

But I have done a thousand dreadful things,
As willingly as one would kill a fly,
And nothing grieves me heartily indeed,
But that I cannot do ten thousand more.

How can you better that hanged man with the scroll pinned upon his breast? Only by carving on dead men's skins your cheerful greetings at their dear friends' door! But the contest is still Marlowe's, even though Shakespeare's grinning monster wins on points, as it were. The agon is renewed in Shakespeare's *King John*, where the dramatist betrays every anxiety at not being comfortable with the mode his play has inherited. With one exception, all the characters goad us to a frenzy of boredom with their Marlovian declamations and lamentations. The particular offender is the dreadful Constance, who famously invokes:

Death, death. O amiable lovely death!
Thou odoriferous stench! sound rottenness!

That first line now reads like a proleptic parody of Walt Whitman. The second sounds like a Max Beerbohm parody of Shakespeare. Out of the ghastly rhetoric of this play, Shakespeare improbably but wonderfully plucks the first of his superb originals, the Bastard Faulconbridge, a powerfully serio-comic misreading of the Marlovian Machiavel, and a giant step upon the way to Falstaff. Shakespeare's daemonic language surges through the beautiful, laughing speeches of the Bastard, who substitutes "commodity" for Marlowe's "policy." The swerve from Marlowe introduces fierce comedy into history, and converts the rhetoric of overreaching into a magnificence of railery. Lewis, the French Dauphin, upon being betrothed to Blanche of Spain, gazes upon the lady with narcissistic satisfaction:

I do protest I never lov'd myself
Till now infixed I beheld myself
Drawn in the flattering table of her eye.

Thrown this gobbet, the Bastard is off and running with it:

> Drawn in the flattering table of her eye!
> Hang'd in the frowning wrinkle of her brow!
> And quarter'd in her heart! he doth espy
> Himself love's traitor. This is pity now,
> That hang'd and drawn and quarter'd there should be
> In such a love so vile a lout as he.

Shakespeare surmounted *King John* in *Richard II*, written two years after Marlowe's death, and directly confronting Marlowe's *Edward II*. Both plays have a royal protagonist, and no hero, but Shakespeare's Richard, though he afflicts us with ambivalence, is a superb lyric poet, while Marlowe's Edward is rather dreary. Like a minor Hamlet, Richard II has faith neither in language nor in himself, nor in anyone else. Unlike Hamlet, this narcissistic monarch is anything but charismatic, and is dominated by considerable masochism. But though he owes some surface colorings to Marlowe's Edward II, he is a psychological labyrinth, a king with the soul of a poet, whereas Edward, as Harry Levin observed, "is a king with the soul of an actor." Shakespeare, who worked hard to become a gentleman commoner, was both poet and actor, and rather severely divides the two by making Bolingbroke, the future Henry IV, assume the quick-change skill of the actor. The theatricality of Edward II is quite showy, but his rhetoric is the emptiest of any prime personage in Marlowe. It is difficult to evade the impression that Marlowe is sadistic towards his Edward, not only in his horrible murder by the ghoul Lightborne but throughout the play. Shakespeare's Richard II, according to Levin, plays his deposition scene even more as an actor than Edward II ever plays, yet that is to undervalue Richard's metaphysical poetry, which sparks and hastens his despair, leaping ahead of Bolingbroke's more circumspect performance. How are we to interpret Shakespeare's audacious allusion to Faustus's Helen, when Richard studies his reflection in the looking-glass he then shatters:

> Was this Face the Face,
> That every day, under his House-hold Roofe,
> Did keep ten thousand men?

Launching a thousand ships and burning the topless towers of Ilium hardly could be more remote from Richard's predicament, or more irrelevant to his rhetorical question. The tag from Marlowe is gratuitous, and however we think Richard intends it, Shakespeare flaunts it as an emblem of his new freedom from Marlowe. Edward II is an aesthete, but not a maker; Richard II is more persuasive in his tragedy because divisions in the self have destroyed him. Edward II loves pleasure, and Gaveston, but is otherwise without personality. Richard II, doom-eager in his destructiveness, is petulant and no more admirable than Edward II, but unlike Edward he has an inner self, and knows too well how to express it.

The major mark of Shakespeare's emancipation from the image of Marlowe is the difference between the two Jews, Barabas and Shylock. Shakespeare's swerve away from his own Marlovian origins gives him, and us, the equivocal triumph of transforming Marlowe's Machiavels into comic heroes, like the Bastard Faulconbridge, or comic villains, like Shylock. I am aware that we do not play Shylock that way, but, alas, we should. René Girard, in his *A Theater of Envy*, rather oddly distinguishes between Barabas, as a supposed reflection of English Renaissance anti-Semitism, and Shylock, as a supposed challenge to that anti-Semitic myth. That gets it the wrong way around: Barabas is at least a grandly entertaining overreacher, akin to Marlowe himself, while all the Christians and Moslems of the play are just as wicked, but not as clever or vitalistic. When Barabas cries out: "Sometimes I go about and poison wells," we scarcely are expected to believe the anti-Semitic myth. Barabas is not Jewish, but Marlovian, and Marlowe is rather more anti-Christian than he is anti-Jewish. But Shakespeare most certainly has written an anti-Semitic masterpiece, one in which the forced conversion of Shylock, at Antonio's insistence, is entirely Shakespeare's own invention, his own shocking addition to the pound-of-flesh story. Indeed, I fear that Shakespeare's revisionary triumph over Marlowe is to give us a psychologically persuasive Jewish devil, rather than the caricature, Barabas. "I'll show you a Jew!" Shakespeare triumphantly implies, while creating a personage far more frightening than Marlowe's cardboard fiend. Shakespeare's creative envy of Marlowe, so long his driving force, has vanished in *The Merchant of Venice.* Barabas is Marlowe, but Shylock has been the Jew throughout four centuries now, and still has great power to hurt.

The coda to Shakespeare's exorcism of Marlowe is neither in Hotspur, who nevertheless is a glorious satire on the Marlovian stance, or in Ancient Pistol's ranting parodies of Tamburlaine. With superb irony, Shakespeare crowds *As You Like It,* least Marlovian of plays, with allusions to Marlowe, all of them decidedly out of context. Overtly, the allusions are to Marlowe's lyric, "The Passionate Shepherd to His Love," or to his unfinished *Hero and Leander,* an Ovidian epyllion. But pragmatically they concern Marlowe's death, and center on the rancid clown Touchstone's wonderful sentence:

> When a man's verses cannot be understood, nor a man's good wit seconded with the forward child, understanding, it strikes a man more dead than a great reckoning in a little room.

The audience could hear in this Barabas's "Infinite riches in a little room," and also a reference to Marlowe's murder in a Deptford tavern, supposedly as a consequence of quarreling over the payment of the bill, "a great reckoning," but evidently at the orders of the royal Secret Service, as Shakespeare may well have known. Charles Nicholl, in his *The Reckoning: The Murder of Christopher Marlowe*, suggests that Shakespeare:

> . . . is saying that when a dead poet's reputation is mishandled and his work misunderstood, as Marlowe's now is, it is like a kind of second death for him.

That seems right to me. Shakespeare, his struggle with poetic influence fully resolved, subtly defends the defamed Marlowe, and in a sense even elegizes him. Yet after the coda, the irony of the epilogue: Edmund in *King Lear*. David Riggs, in his *Ben Jonson: A Life*, confirms John Hollander's intuition that Malvolio in *Twelfth Night* is, to some degree, a satire upon Jonson, the "purge" administered by Shakespeare to Jonson that is spoken of in *The Return from Parnassus, Part II*. Edmund is far more than a satire upon anyone; he is a subtle refinement upon Iago, and perhaps the greater villain, with even more acute intelligence and with an icier contempt for all his victims. But his nihilism, his charm, his genius, his "atheism," his frightening freedom from all constraints, his powers of rhetorical persuasion, his refusal to be hypocritical, unlike his mistresses, Goneril and Regan, suggest Marlowe. In some respects the Bastard Edmund is a darker version of the Bastard Faulconbridge, but with the familial loyalty and patriotism inverted to their treasonous opposites. Unlike Jonson-as-Malvolio, Marlowe-as-Edmund cannot be supported by external evidence, at least in the present state of our knowledge. Yet, as a creative "misreading" or misprision of Marlowe's actual personality and character, the Edmund of *King Lear* is Shakespeare's final, equivocal tribute to his precursor's Machiavels.

We have no direct path into what is central in Shakespeare, because he is a larger form of thought, of language,

and of feeling than any other we can come to know. It
is not that the greatest of his plays *are* plays; we are not
blocked from surmising what may be central in Marlowe
or in Jonson. With all their difficulties, Dante and Milton
and Wordsworth seem to yield many of their secrets to us,
if we but read them incessantly and with all our ardor. But
Shakespeare, while entertaining us at every possible level,
never permits us voyage to the undiscovered country of his
self. Borges thought that Shakespeare was selfless, and there-
fore Shakespeare was everyman. What we insist upon call-
ing "theory" dogmatizes that no one ever had or ever will
have a self of her or his own. That seems to me an unami-
able fiction. Is it only a Borgesian or amiable fiction to say
that Shakespeare is at once everyone and no one? Shake-
speare thought enough of his friend Ben Jonson to satirize
him as Malvolio, and was haunted enough by his acquain-
tance Christopher Marlowe to portray him, with marvelous
ambivalence, as Edmund. Did Shakespeare not feel concern
enough, interest and esteem enough, for himself, to put that
self on stage? He acted old men, or kings, or ghosts. Does
the Player-King in *Hamlet* speak for Shakespeare, or for
Hamlet? Is the survivor Edgar in some sense a representa-
tion of the survivor Shakespeare? Oscar Wilde might have
been interested in questions like these; no living scholar-
critic of Shakespeare would allow them. James Joyce, like
some others before and since, identified Hamlet with
Hamnet Shakespeare, the dramatist's only son, dead at
eleven. More than any other play by Shakespeare (or by
anyone else), *Hamlet* is an endless provocation to the world,
because the world has found an unsolved mystery in it.
A writer boundless to our meditation, Shakespeare never-
theless seems not to have cared to direct that meditation.
I know of only one strong clue to Shakespeare's track-
lessness: his long harboring of the image of Marlowe. Ovid
and Chaucer were safely remote in time; the forerunner

Marlowe was born just two months before Shakespeare, who survived Marlowe by twenty-three years.

If Marlowe, to Shakespeare, primarily was an image of the poet's dangerous freedom and of the playwright's dangerous power over an audience, then the image would have sufficed, and Shakespeare might have been content to repeat himself, once he had emancipated himself with Falstaff, Hamlet, and Rosalind. Some scholars argue that Shakespeare moved from tragedy to what we call "romance" because of commercial pressure from rival dramatists. Shakespeare would take from anyone and everywhere, with both fists, but his daemon or genius drove him, after he had triumphed over Marlowe. Change, the only law observed by his protagonists, was also the law of Shakespeare's inwardness. All fictions aside, I cannot see anyone representing an infinitely growing inner self, without knowing it in all immediacy. There is very little change in Marlowe: all his vaunters are one vaunter, his victims one victim, his Machiavels one Nick. Tamburlaine, Barabas, the Guise, even Faustus share the same rhetoric, and are dizzy with the same desires. Shakespeare, swerving from Marlowe, created distincts. Poetic influence has no greater triumph.

THE ANXIETY OF INFLUENCE

PROLOGUE

It Was A Great Marvel That They Were In The Father Without Knowing Him

After he knew that he had fallen, outwards and downwards, away from the Fullness, he tried to remember what the Fullness had been.

He did remember, but found he was silent, and could not tell the others.

He wanted to tell them that she leapt farthest forward and fell into a passion apart from his embrace.

She was in great agony, and would have been swallowed up by the sweetness, had she not reached a limit, and stopped.

But the passion went on without her, and passed beyond the limit.

Sometimes he thought he was about to speak, but the silence continued.

He wanted to say: "strengthless and female fruit."

> . . . A more severe,
>
> More harassing master would extemporize
> Subtler, more urgent proof that the theory
> Of poetry is the theory of life,
>
> As it is, in the intricate evasions of as. . . .

STEVENS, *An Ordinary Evening in New Haven*

INTRODUCTION

*A Meditation upon Priority,
and a Synopsis*

This short book offers a theory of poetry by way of a description of poetic influence, or the story of intra-poetic relationships. One aim of this theory is corrective: to de-idealize our accepted accounts of how one poet helps to form another. Another aim, also corrective, is to try to provide a poetics that will foster a more adequate practical criticism.

Poetic history, in this book's argument, is held to be indistinguishable from poetic influence, since strong poets make that history by misreading one another, so as to clear imaginative space for themselves.

My concern is only with strong poets, major figures with the persistence to wrestle with their strong precursors, even to the death. Weaker talents idealize; figures of capable imagination appropriate for themselves. But nothing is got for nothing, and self-appropriation involves the immense anxieties of indebtedness, for what strong maker desires the realization that he has failed to create himself? Oscar Wilde, who knew he had failed as a poet because he lacked strength to overcome his anxiety of influence, knew also the darker truths concerning influence. *The Ballad of Reading Gaol* becomes an embarrassment to read, directly one recognizes that every lustre it exhibits is reflected from *The Rime of the Ancient Mariner;* and Wilde's lyrics anthologize the whole of English High Romanticism. Knowing this, and armed with his customary intelligence, Wilde bitterly remarks in *The Portrait of Mr. W. H.* that: "Influence is simply a transference of personality, a mode of giving away what is most precious to one's self, and its exercise produces a sense, and, it may be, a reality of loss. Every disciple takes away something from his master." This is the anxiety of influencing, yet no reversal in this area is a true reversal. Two years later, Wilde refined this bitterness in one of Lord Henry Wotton's elegant observations in *The Picture of Dorian Gray,* where he tells Dorian that all influence is immoral:

> Because to influence a person is to give him one's own soul. He does not think his natural thoughts, or burn with his natural passions. His virtues are not real to him. His sins, if there are such things as sins, are borrowed. He becomes an echo of someone else's music, an actor of a part that has not been written for him.

To apply Lord Henry's insight to Wilde, we need only read Wilde's review of Pater's *Appreciations,* with its splendidly self-deceptive closing observation that Pater "has escaped disciples." Every major aesthetic consciousness seems peculiarly more gifted at denying obligation as the hungry generations go on treading one another down. Stevens, a stronger heir of Pater than even Wilde was, is revealingly vehement in his letters:

> While, of course, I come down from the past, the past is my own and not something marked Coleridge, Wordsworth,

etc. I know of no one who has been particularly important to me. My reality-imagination complex is entirely my own even though I see it in others.

He might have said: "particularly because I see it in others," but poetic influence was hardly a subject where Stevens' insights could center. Towards the end, his denials became rather violent, and oddly humored. Writing to the poet Richard Eberhart, he extends a sympathy all the stronger for being self-sympathy:

> I sympathize with your denial of any influence on my part. This sort of thing always jars me because, in my own case, I am not conscious of having been influenced by anybody and have purposely held off from reading highly mannered people like Eliot and Pound so that I should not absorb anything, even unconsciously. But there is a kind of critic who spends his time dissecting what he reads for echoes, imitations, influences, as if no one was ever simply himself but is always compounded of a lot of other people. As for W. Blake, I think that this means Wilhelm Blake.

This view, that poetic influence scarcely exists, except in furiously active pedants, is itself an illustration of one way in which poetic influence is a variety of melancholy or an anxiety-principle. Stevens was, as he insisted, a highly individual poet, as much an American original as Whitman or Dickinson, or his own contemporaries: Pound, Williams, Moore. But poetic influence need not make poets less original; as often it makes them more original, though not therefore necessarily better. The profundities of poetic influence cannot be reduced to source-study, to the history of ideas, to the patterning of images. Poetic influence, or as I shall more frequently term it, poetic misprision, is necessarily the study of the life-cycle of the poet-as-poet. When such study considers the context in which that life-cycle is enacted, it will be compelled to examine simultaneously the relations between poets as cases akin to what Freud called the family romance, and as chapters in the history of modern revisionism, "modern" meaning here post-Enlightenment. The modern poet, as W. J. Bate shows in *The Burden of the Past and the English Poet,* is the inheritor of a melancholy engendered in the mind of the Enlightenment by its skepticism of its own double heritage of imaginative wealth, from the ancients and from the Renaissance masters. In this book I largely neglect the area Bate has explored with great skill, in order to center upon intra-poetic relationships as parallels of family romance. Though I employ these parallels, I do so as a deliberate revisionist of some of the Freudian emphases.

Nietzsche and Freud are, so far as I can tell, the prime influences upon the theory of influence presented in this book. Nietzsche is the prophet of the antithetical, and his *Genealogy of Morals* is the profoundest study available to me of the revisionary and ascetic strains in the aesthetic temperament. Freud's investigations of the mechanisms of defense and their ambivalent functionings provide the clearest analogues I have found for the revisionary ratios that govern intra-poetic relations. Yet, the theory of influence expounded here is un-Nietzschean in its deliberate literalism, and in its Viconian insistence that priority in divination is crucial for every strong poet, lest he dwindle merely into a latecomer. My theory rejects also the qualified Freudian optimism that happy substitution is possible, that a second chance can save us from the repetitive quest for our earliest attachments. Poets as poets cannot accept substitutions, and fight to the end to have their initial chance alone. Both Nietzsche and Freud underestimated poets and poetry, yet each yielded more power to phantasmagoria than it truly possesses. They too, despite their moral realism, over-idealized the imagination. Nietzsche's disciple, Yeats, and Freud's disciple, Otto Rank, show a greater awareness of the artist's fight against art, and of the relation of this struggle to the artist's antithetical battle against nature.

Freud recognized sublimation as the highest human achievement, a recognition that allies him to Plato and to the entire moral traditions of both Judaism and Christianity. Freudian sublimation involves the yielding-up of more primordial for more refined modes of pleasure, which is to exalt the second chance above the first. Freud's poem, in the view of this book, is not severe enough, unlike the severe poems written by the creative lives of the strong poets. To equate emotional maturation with the discovery of acceptable substitutes may be pragmatic wisdom, particularly in the realm of Eros, but this is not the wisdom of the strong poets. The surrendered dream is not merely a phantasmagoria of endless gratification, but is the greatest of all human illusions, the vision of immortality. If Wordsworth's *Ode: Intimations of Immortality from Recollections of Early Childhood* possessed only the wisdom found also in Freud, then we could cease calling it "the Great Ode." Wordsworth too saw repetition or second chance as essential for development, and his ode admits that we can redirect our needs by substitution or sublimation. But the ode plangently also awakens into failure, and into the creative mind's protest against time's tyranny. A Wordsworthian critic, even one as loyal to Wordsworth as Geoffrey Hartman, can insist upon clearly distinguishing between *priority*, as a concept from the natural order, and *authority*, from the spiritual order, but Wordsworth's ode declines to make this distinction. "By seeking to overcome priority," Hartman wisely says, "art fights nature on nature's own ground, and is bound to lose." The argument of this book is that strong poets are condemned to just this unwisdom; Wordsworth's Great Ode fights nature on nature's own ground, and suffers a great defeat, even as it retains its greater dream. That dream, in Wordsworth's ode, is shadowed by the anxiety of influence, due to the greatness of the precursor-poem, Milton's *Lycidas,* where the human refusal wholly to sublimate is even more rugged, despite the ostensible yielding to Christian teachings of sublimation.

For every poet begins (however "unconsciously") by rebelling more strongly against the consciousness of death's necessity than all other men and women do. The young citizen of poetry, or ephebe as Athens would have called him, is already the anti-natural or antithetical man, and from his start as a poet he quests for an impossible object, as his precursor quested before him. That this quest encompasses necessarily the diminishment of poetry seems to me an inevitable realization, one that accurate literary history must sustain. The great poets of the English Renaissance are not matched by their Enlightened descendants, and the whole tradition of the post-Enlightenment, which is Romanticism, shows a further decline in its Modernist and post-Modernist heirs. The death of poetry will not be hastened by any reader's broodings, yet it seems just to assume that poetry in our tradition, when it dies, will be self-slain, murdered by its own past strength. An implied anguish throughout this book is that Romanticism, for all its glories, may have been a vast visionary tragedy, the self-baffled enterprise not of Prometheus but of blinded Oedipus, who did not know that the Sphinx was his Muse.

Oedipus, blind, was on the path to oracular godhood, and the strong poets have followed him by transforming their blindness towards their precursors into the revisionary insights of their own work. The six revisionary movements that I will trace in the strong poet's life-cycle could as well be more, and could take quite different names than those I have employed. I have kept them to six, because these seem to be minimal and essential to my understanding of how one poet deviates from another. The names, though arbitrary, carry on from various traditions that have been central in Western imaginative life, and I hope can be useful.

The greatest poet in our language is excluded from the argument of this book for several reasons. One is necessarily historical; Shakespeare belongs to the giant age before the flood, before the anxiety of influence became central to poetic consciousness. Another has to do with the contrast between dramatic and lyric form. As poetry has become more subjective, the shadow cast by the precursors has become more dominant. The main cause, though, is that Shakespeare's prime precursor was Marlowe, a poet very much smaller than his inheritor. Milton, with all his strength, yet had to struggle, subtly and crucially, with a major precursor in Spenser, and this struggle both formed and malformed Milton. Coleridge, ephebe of Milton and later of Wordsworth, would have been glad to find his Marlowe in Cowper (or in the much weaker Bowles), but influence cannot be willed. Shakespeare is the largest instance in the language of a phenomenon that stands outside the concern of this book: the absolute absorption of the precursor. Battle between strong equals, father and son as mighty opposites, Laius and Oedipus at the crossroads; only this is my subject here, though some of the fathers, as will be seen, are composite figures. That even the strongest poets are subject to influences not poetical is obvious even to me, but again my concern is only with *the poet in a poet,* or the aboriginal poetic self.

A change like the one I propose in our ideas of influence should help us read more accurately any group of past poets who were contemporary with one another. To give one example, as misinterpreters of Keats, *in their poems,* the Victorian disciples of Keats most notably include Tennyson, Arnold, Hopkins, and Rossetti. That Tennyson triumphed in his long, hidden contest with Keats, no one can assert absolutely, but his clear superiority over Arnold, Hopkins, and Rossetti is due to his relative victory or at least holding of his own in contrast to their partial defeats. Arnold's elegiac poetry uneasily blends Keatsian style with anti-Romantic sentiment, while Hopkins' strained intensities and convolutions of diction and Rossetti's densely inlaid art are also at variance with the burdens they seek to alleviate in their own poetic selves. Similarly, in our time we need to look again at Pound's unending match with Browning, as at Stevens' long and largely hidden civil war with the major poets of English and American Romanticism—Wordsworth, Keats, Shelley, Emerson, and Whitman. As with the Victorian Keatsians, these are instances among many, if a more accurate story is to be told about poetic history.

This book's main purpose is necessarily to present one reader's critical vision, in the context both of the criticism and poetry of his own generation, where their current crises most touch him, and in the context of his own anxieties of influence. In the contemporary poems that most move me, like the *Corsons Inlet* and *Saliences* of A. R. Ammons and the *Fragment* and *Soonest Mended* of John Ashbery, I can recognize a strength that battles against the death of poetry, yet also the exhaustions of being a latecomer. Similarly, in the contemporary criticism that clarifies for me my own evasions, in books like *Allegory* by Angus Fletcher, *Beyond Formalism* by Geoffrey Hartman, and *Blindness and Insight* by Paul de Man, I am made aware of the mind's effort to overcome the impasse of Formalist criticism, the barren moralizing that Archetypal criticism has come to be, and the anti-humanistic plain dreariness of all those developments in European criticism that have yet to demonstrate that they can aid in reading any one poem by any poet whatsoever. My Interchapter, proposing a more antithetical practical criticism than any we now have, is my response in this area of the contemporary.

A theory of poetry that presents itself as a severe poem, reliant upon aphorism, apothegm, and a quite personal (though thoroughly traditional) mythic pattern, still may be judged, and may ask to be judged, as argument. Everything that makes up this book—parables, definitions, the working-through of the revisionary ratios as mechanisms of defense—intends to be part of a unified meditation on the melancholy of the creative mind's desperate insistence upon priority. Vico, who read all creation as a severe poem, understood that priority in the natural order and authority in the spiritual order had been one and had to remain one, *for poets,* because only this harshness constituted Poetic Wisdom. Vico reduced both natural priority and spiritual authority to property, a Hermetic reduction that I recognize as the *Ananke,* the dreadful necessity still governing the Western imagination.

Valentinus, second-century Gnostic speculator, came out of Alexandria to teach the Pleroma, the Fullness of thirty Aeons, manifold of Divinity: "It was a great marvel that they were in the Father without knowing Him." To search for where you already are is the most benighted of quests, and the most fated. Each strong poet's Muse, his Sophia, leaps as far out and down as can be, in a solipsistic passion of quest. Valentinus posited a Limit, at which quest ends, but no quest ends, if its context is Unconditioned Mind, the cosmos of the greatest post-Miltonic poets. The Sophia of Valentinus recovered, wed again within the Pleroma, and only her Passion or Dark Intention was separated out into our world, beyond the Limit.

Into this Passion, the Dark Intention that Valentinus called "strengthless and female fruit," the ephebe must fall. If he emerges from it, however crippled and blinded, he will be among the strong poets.

SYNOPSIS: SIX REVISIONARY RATIOS

1. *Clinamen,* which is poetic misreading or misprision proper; I take the word from Lucretius, where it means a "swerve" of the atoms so as to make change possible in the universe. A poet swerves away from his precursor, by so reading his precursor's poem as to execute a *clinamen* in relation to it. This appears as a corrective movement in his own poem, which implies that the precursor poem went accurately up to a certain point, but then should have swerved, precisely in the direction that the new poem moves.

2. *Tessera,* which is completion and antithesis; I take the word not from mosaic-making, where it is still used, but from the ancient mystery cults, where it meant a token of recognition, the fragment say of a small pot which with the other fragments would re-constitute the vessel. A poet antithetically "completes" his precursor, by so reading the parent-poem as to retain its terms but to mean them in another sense, as though the precursor had failed to go far enough.

3. *Kenosis,* which is a breaking-device similar to the defense mechanisms our psyches employ against repetition compulsions; *kenosis* then is a movement towards discontinuity with the precursor. I take the word from St. Paul, where it means the humbling or emptying-out of Jesus by himself, when he accepts reduction from divine to human status. The later poet, apparently emptying himself of his own afflatus, his imaginative godhood, seems to humble

himself as though he were ceasing to be a poet, but this ebbing is so performed in relation to a precursor's poem-of-ebbing that the precursor is emptied out also, and so the later poem of deflation is not as absolute as it seems.

4. *Daemonization,* or a movement towards a personal-ized Counter-Sublime, in reaction to the precursor's Sub-lime; I take the term from general Neo-Platonic usage, where an intermediary being, neither divine nor human, enters into the adept to aid him. The later poet opens himself to what he believes to be a power in the parent-poem that does not belong to the parent proper, but to a range of being just beyond that precursor. He does this, in his poem, by so stationing its relation to the parent-poem as to generalize away the uniqueness of the earlier work.

5. *Askesis,* or a movement of self-purgation which in-tends the attainment of a state of solitude; I take the term, general as it is, particularly from the practice of pre-Socra-tic shamans like Empedocles. The later poet does not, as in *kenosis,* undergo a revisionary movement of emptying, but of curtailing; he yields up part of his own human and imaginative endowment, so as to separate himself from others, including the precursor, and he does this in his poem by so stationing it in regard to the parent-poem as to make that poem undergo an *askesis* too; the precursor's endowment is also truncated.

6. *Apophrades,* or the return of the dead; I take the word from the Athenian dismal or unlucky days upon which the dead returned to reinhabit the houses in which they had lived. The later poet, in his own final phase, al-ready burdened by an imaginative solitude that is almost a solipsism, holds his own poem so open again to the pre-cursor's work that at first we might believe the wheel has

come full circle, and that we are back in the later poet's flooded apprenticeship, before his strength began to assert itself in the revisionary ratios. But the poem is now *held* open to the precursor, where once it *was* open, and the uncanny effect is that the new poem's achievement makes it seem to us, not as though the precursor were writing it, but as though the later poet himself had written the precursor's characteristic work.

One

. . . when you consider
the radiance, that it will look into the guiltiest
swervings of the weaving heart and bear itself upon them,
not flinching into disguise or darkening. . . .

A. R. AMMONS

Clinamen

or POETIC MISPRISION

Shelley speculated that poets of all ages contributed to one Great Poem perpetually in progress. Borges remarks that poets create their precursors. If the dead poets, as Eliot insisted, constituted their successors' particular advance in knowledge, that knowledge is still their successors' creation, made by the living for the needs of the living.

But poets, or at least the strongest among them, do not read necessarily as even the strongest of critics read. Poets are neither ideal nor common readers, neither Arnoldian nor Johnsonian. They tend not to think, as they read: "This is dead, this is living, in the poetry of X." Poets, by the time they have grown strong, do not read the poetry of X, for really strong poets can read only themselves. For them, to be judicious is to be weak, and to compare, exactly and fairly, is to be not elect. Milton's Satan, archetype of the modern poet at his strongest, becomes weak when he reasons and compares, on Mount Niphates, and so commences that process of decline culminating in *Para-*

dise Regained, ending as the archetype of the modern critic at his weakest.

Let us attempt the experiment (apparently frivolous) of reading *Paradise Lost* as an allegory of the dilemma of the modern poet, at his strongest. Satan is that modern poet, while God is his dead but still embarrassingly potent and present ancestor, or rather, ancestral poet. Adam is the potentially strong modern poet, but at his weakest moment, when he has yet to find his own voice. God has no Muse, and needs none, since he is dead, his creativity being manifested only in the past time of the poem. Of the living poets in the poem, Satan has Sin, Adam has Eve, and Milton has only his Interior Paramour, an Emanation far within that weeps incessantly for his sin, and that is invoked magnificently four times in the poem. Milton has no name for her, though he invokes her under several; but, as he says, "the meaning, not the Name I call." Satan, a stronger poet even than Milton, has progressed beyond invoking his Muse.

Why call Satan a modern poet? Because he shadows forth gigantically a trouble at the core of Milton and of Pope, a sorrow that purifies by isolation in Collins and Gray, in Smart and in Cowper, emerging fully to stand clear in Wordsworth, who is the exemplary Modern Poet, the Poet proper. The incarnation of the Poetic Character in Satan begins when Milton's story truly begins, with the Incarnation of God's Son and Satan's rejection of *that* incarnation. Modern poetry begins in two declarations of Satan: "We know no time when we were not as now" and "To be weak is miserable, doing or suffering."

Let us adopt Milton's own sequence in the poem. Poetry begins with our awareness, not of a Fall, but that *we are falling.* The poet is our chosen man, and his consciousness of election comes as a curse; again, not "I am a fallen man," but "I am Man, and I am falling"—or rather, "I *was* God, I *was* Man (for to a poet they were the same), and I *am* falling, from myself." When this consciousness of self is raised to an absolute pitch, *then* the poet hits the floor of Hell, or rather, comes to the bottom of the abyss, and by his impact there creates Hell. He says, "I seem to have stopped falling; now I *am fallen,* consequently, I lie here in Hell."

There and then, in this bad, he finds his good; he chooses the heroic, to know damnation and to explore the limits of the possible within it. The alternative is to repent, to accept a God altogether other than the self, wholly external to the possible. This God is cultural history, the dead poets, the embarrassments of a traditon grown too wealthy to need anything more. But we, to understand the strong poet, must go further still than he can go, back into the poise before the consciousness of falling came.

When Satan or the poet looks around him on the floor of fire his falling self had kindled, he sees first a face he only just recognizes, his best friend, Beelzebub, or the talented poet who never quite made it, and now never shall. And, like the truly strong poet he is, Satan is interested in the face of his best friend only to the extent that it reveals to him the condition of his own countenance. Such limited interest mocks neither the poets we know, nor the truly heroic Satan. If Beelzebub is that scarred, if he looks that unlike the true form he left behind on the happy fields of light, then Satan himself is hideously bereft of beauty, doomed, like Walter Pater, to be a Caliban of Letters, trapped in essential poverty, in imaginative need, where once he was all but the wealthiest, and needed next to nothing. But Satan, in the accursed strength of the poet, refuses to brood upon this, and turns instead to his task, which is to rally everything that remains.

This task, comprehensive and profoundly imaginative,

includes everything that we could ascribe as motivation for the writing of any poetry that is not strictly devotional in its purposes. For why do men write poems? To rally everything that remains, and not to sanctify nor propound. The heroism of endurance—of Milton's post-lapsarian Adam, and of the Son in *Paradise Regained*—is a theme for Christian poetry, but only barely a heroism for poets. We hear Milton again, celebrating the strong poet's natural virtue, when Samson taunts Harapha: "bring up thy van,/ My heels are fetter'd, but my fist is free." The poet's final heroism, in Milton, is a spasm of self-destruction, glorious because it pulls down the temple of his enemies. Satan, organizing his chaos, imposing a discipline despite the visible darkness, calling his minions to emulate his refusal to mourn, becomes the hero as poet, finding what must suffice, while knowing that nothing can suffice.

This is a heroism that is exactly on the border of solipsism, neither within it, nor beyond it. Satan's later decline in the poem, as arranged by the Idiot Questioner in Milton, is that the hero retreats from this border into solipsism, and so is degraded; ceases, during his soliloquy on Mount Niphates, to be a poet and, by intoning the formula: "Evil be thou my good," becomes a mere rebel, a childish inverter of conventional moral categories, another wearisome ancestor of student non-students, the perpetual New Left. For the modern poet, in the gladness of his sorrowing strength, stands always on the farther verge of solipsism, having just emerged from it. His difficult balance, from Wordsworth to Stevens, is to maintain a stance just there, where by his very presence he says: "What I see and hear come not but from myself" and yet also: "I have not but I am and as I am I am." The first, by itself, is perhaps the fine defiance of an overt solipsism, leading back to an equivalent of "I know no time when I was not as now." Yet the second is the modification that makes for poetry instead of idiocy: "There are no objects outside of me because I see into their life, which is one with my own, and so 'I am that I am,' which is to say, 'I too will be present wherever and whenever I choose to be present.' I am so much in process, that all possible movement is indeed possible, and if at present I explore only my own dens, at least I *explore*." Or, as Satan might have said: "In doing and in suffering, I shall be happy, for even in suffering I shall be strong."

It is sad to observe most modern critics observing Satan, because they never do observe him. The catalog of unseeing could hardly be more distinguished, from Eliot who speaks of "Milton's curly haired Byronic hero" (one wants to reply, looking from side to side: "Who?") to the astonishing backsliding of Northrop Frye, who invokes, in urbane ridicule, a Wagnerian context (one wants to lament: "A true critic, and of God's party without knowing it"). Fortunately we have had Empson, with his apt rallying cry: "Back to Shelley!" Whereto I go.

Contemplating Milton's meanness towards Satan, towards his rival poet and dark brother, Shelley spoke of the "pernicious casuistry" set up in the mind of Milton's reader, who would be tempted to weigh Satan's flaws against God's malice towards him, and to excuse Satan because God had been malicious beyond all measure. Shelley's point has been twisted by the C. S. Lewis or Angelic School of Milton Criticism, who proceed to weigh up the flaws and God's wrongs, and find Satan wanting in the balance. This pernicious casuistry, Shelley would have agreed, would not be less pernicious if we were to find (as I do) Milton's God wanting. It would still be casuistry, and as discourse upon poetry it would still be moralizing, which is to say, pernicious.

Even the strongest poets were at first weak, for they

started as prospective Adams, not as retrospective Satans. Blake names one state of being Adam, and calls it the Limit of Contraction, and another state Satan, and calls it the Limit of Opacity. Adam is given or natural man, beyond which our imaginations will not contract. Satan is the thwarted or restrained desire of natural man, or rather the shadow or Spectre of that desire. Beyond this spectral state, we will not harden against vision, but the Spectre squats in our repressiveness, and we are hardened enough, as we are contracted enough. Enough, our spirits lament, not to live our lives, enough to be frightened out of our creative potential by the Covering Cherub, Blake's emblem (out of Milton, and Ezekiel, and Genesis) for that portion of creativity in us that has gone over to constriction and hardness. Blake precisely named this renegade part of Man. Before the Fall (which for Blake meant before the Creation, the two events for him being one and the same) the Covering Cherub was the pastoral genius Tharmas, a unifying process making for undivided consciousness; the innocence, pre-reflective, of a state without subjects and objects, yet in no danger of solipsism, for it lacked also a consciousness of self. Tharmas is a poet's (or any man's) power of realization, even as the Covering Cherub is the power that blocks realization.

No poet, not even one so single-minded as Milton or Wordsworth, is a Tharmas, this late in history, and no poet is a Covering Cherub, though Coleridge and Hopkins both allowed themselves, at last, to be dominated by him, as perhaps Eliot did also. Poets this late in tradition are both Adams and Satans. They begin as natural men, affirming that they will contract no further, and they end as thwarted desires, frustrated only that they cannot harden apocalyptically. But, in between, the greatest of them are very strong, and they progress through a natural intensification that marks Adam in his brief prime and a heroic self-realization that marks Satan in his brief and more-than-natural glory. The intensification and the self-realization alike are accomplished only through language, and no poet since Adam and Satan speaks a language free of the one wrought by his precursors. Chomsky remarks that when one speaks a language, one knows a great deal that was never learned. The effort of criticism is to teach a language, for what is never learned but comes as the gift of a language is a poetry already written—an insight I derive from Shelley's remark that every language is the relic of an abandoned cyclic poem. I mean that criticism teaches not a language of criticism (a formalist view still held in common by archetypalists, structuralists, and phenomenologists) but a language in which poetry already is written, the language of influence, of the dialectic that governs the relations between poets *as poets.* The poet *in every reader* does not experience the same disjunction from what he reads that the critic in every reader necessarily feels. What gives pleasure to the critic in a reader may give anxiety to the poet in him, an anxiety we have learned, as readers, to neglect, to our own loss and peril. This anxiety, this mode of melancholy, is the anxiety of influence, the dark and daemonic ground upon which we now enter.

How do men become poets, or to adopt an older phrasing, how is the poetic character incarnated? When a potential poet first discovers (or is discovered by) the dialectic of influence, first discovers poetry as being both external and internal to himself, he begins a process that will end only when he has no more poetry within him, long after he has the power (or desire) to discover it outside himself again. Though all such discovery is a self-recognition, indeed a Second Birth, and ought, in the pure good of theory, to be accomplished in a perfect solipsism, it is an act never complete in itself. Poetic Influence in the sense—amazing, agonizing, delighting—of *other poets,* as felt in the depths of the all but perfect solipsist, the potentially strong poet. For the poet is condemned to learn his profoundest yearnings through an awareness of *other selves.* The poem is *within* him, yet he experiences the shame and splendor of *being found by* poems—great poems—*outside* him. To lose freedom in this center is never to forgive, and to learn the dread of threatened autonomy forever.

"Every young man's heart," Malraux says, "is a graveyard in which are inscribed the names of a thousand dead artists but whose only actual denizens are a few mighty, often antagonistic, ghosts." "The poet," Malraux adds, "is haunted by a voice with which words must be harmonized." As his main concerns are visual and narrative, Malraux arrives at the formula: "from pastiche to style," which is not adequate for poetic influence, where the movement toward self-realization is closer to the more drastic spirit of Kierkegaard's maxim: "He who is willing to work gives birth to his own father." We remember how for so many centuries, from the sons of Homer to the sons of Ben Jonson, poetic influence had been described as a filial relationship, and then we come to see that poetic *influence,* rather than *sonship,* is another product of the Enlightenment, another aspect of the Cartesian dualism.

The word "influence" had received the sense of "having a power over another" as early as the Scholastic Latin of Aquinas, but not for centuries was it to lose its root meaning of "inflow," and its prime meaning of an emanation or force coming in upon mankind from the stars. As first used, to be influenced meant to receive an ethereal fluid flowing in upon one from the stars, a fluid that affected one's character and destiny, and that altered all sublunary things. A power—divine and moral—later simply a secret power—exercised itself, in defiance of all that had seemed

voluntary in one. In our sense—that of *poetic* influence
—the word is very late. In English it is not one of Dry-
den's critical terms, and is never used in our sense by
Pope. Johnson in 1755 defines influence as being either
astral or moral, saying of the latter that it is "Ascendant
power; power of directing or modifying"; but the in-
stances he cites are religious or personal, and not literary.
For Coleridge, two generations later, the word has sub-
stantially our meaning in the context of literature.

But the anxiety had long preceded the usage. Between
Ben Jonson and Samuel Johnson filial loyalty between
poets had given way to the labyrinthine affections of what
Freud's wit first termed the "family romance," and moral
power had become a legacy of melancholy. Ben Jonson
still sees influence as health. Of *imitation,* he says he
means: "to be able to convert the substance or riches of
another poet to his own use. To make choice of one excel-
lent man above the rest, and so to follow him till he grow
very he, or so like him as the copy may be mistaken for
the original." So Ben Jonson has no anxiety as to imita-
tion, for to him (refreshingly) art is *hard work.* But the
shadow fell, and with the post-Enlightenment passion for
Genius and the Sublime, there came anxiety too, for art
was beyond hard work. Edward Young, with his Lon-
ginian esteem for *Genius,* broods on the baneful virtues of
the poetic fathers and anticipates the Keats of the letters
and the Emerson of *Self-Reliance* when he laments, of the
great precursors: "They *engross* our attention, and so pre-
vent a due inspection of ourselves; they *prejudice* our
judgment in favor of their abilities, and so lessen the sense
of our own; and they *intimidate* us with this splendor of
their renown." And Dr. Samuel Johnson, a sturdier man
and with more classical loyalties, nevertheless created a
complex critical matrix in which the notions of indolence,
solitude, originality, imitation, and invention are most

strangely mixed. Johnson barked: "The case of Tantalus, in the region of poetick punishment, was somewhat to be pitied, because the fruits that hung about him retired from his hand; but what tenderness can be claimed by those who though perhaps they suffer the pains of Tantalus will never lift their hands for their own relief?" We wince at the Johnsonian bow-wow, and wince the more because we know he means himself as well, for as a poet he was another Tantalus, another victim of the Covering Cherub. In this respect, only Shakespeare and Milton escaped a Johnsonian whipping; even Virgil was condemned as too much a mere imitator of Homer. For, with Johnson, the greatest critic in the language, we have also the first great diagnostician of the malady of poetic influence. Yet the diagnosis belongs to his age. Hume, who admired Waller, thought Waller was saved only because Horace was so distant. We are further on, and see that Horace was not distant enough. Waller is dead. Horace lives. "The burden of government," Johnson brooded, "is increased upon princes by the virtues of their immediate predecessors," and he added: "He that succeeds a celebrated writer, has the same difficulties to encounter." We know the rancid humor of this too well, and any reader of *Advertisements For Myself* may enjoy the frantic dances of Norman Mailer as he strives to evade his own anxiety that it is, after all, Hemingway all the way. Or, less enjoyably, we can read through Roethke's *The Far Field* or Berryman's *His Toy, His Dream, His Rest,* and discover the field alas is too near to those of Whitman, Eliot, Stevens, Yeats, and the toy, dream, veritable rest are also the comforts of the same poets. Influence, for us, is the anxiety it was to Johnson and Hume, but the pathos lengthens as the dignity diminishes in this story.

Poetic Influence, as time has tarnished it, is part of the larger phenomenon of intellectual revisionism. And revisionism, whether in political theory, psychology, theology, law, poetics, has changed its nature in our time. The ancestor of revisionism is heresy, but heresy tended to change received doctrine by an alteration of balances, rather than by what could be called creative correction, the more particular mark of modern revisionism. Heresy resulted, generally, from a change in emphasis, while revisionism follows received doctrine along to a certain point, and then deviates, insisting that a wrong direction was taken at just that point, and no other. Freud, contemplating his revisionists, murmured: "You have only to think of the strong emotional factors that make it hard for many people to fit themselves in with others or to subordinate themselves," but Freud was too tactful to analyze just those "strong emotional factors." Blake, happily free of such tact, remains the most profound and original theorist of revisionism to appear since the Enlightenment and an inevitable aid in the development of a new theory of Poetic Influence. To be enslaved by any precursor's system, Blake says, is to be inhibited from creativity by an obsessive reasoning and comparing, presumably of one's own works to the precursor's. Poetic Influence is thus a disease of self-consciousness; but Blake was not released from his share in that anxiety. What plagued him, a litany of evils, came to him most powerfully in his vision of the greatest of his precursors:

> . . . the Male-Females, the Dragon Forms,
> Religion hid in War, a Dragon red & hidden Harlot.

> All these are seen in Milton's Shadow, who is the Covering
>   Cherub. . . .

We know, as Blake did, that Poetic Influence is gain and loss, inseparably wound in the labyrinth of history. What is the nature of the gain? Blake distinguished be-

tween States and Individuals. Individuals passed through
States of Being, and remained Individuals, but States were
always in process, always shifting. And only States were
culpable, Individuals never. Poetic Influence is a passing
of Individuals or Particulars through States. Like all revi-
sionism, Poetic Influence is a gift of the spirit that comes
to us only through what could be called, dispassionately,
the perversity of the spirit, or what Blake more accurately
judged the perversity of States.

It does happen that one poet influences another, or
more precisely, that one poet's poems influence the poems
of the other, through a generosity of the spirit, even a
shared generosity. But our easy idealism is out of place
here. Where generosity is involved, the poets influenced
are minor or weaker; the more generosity, and the more
mutual it is, the poorer the poets involved. And here also,
the influencing moves by way of misapprehension, though
this tends to be indeliberate and almost unconscious. I ar-
rive at my argument's central principle, which is not more
true for its outrageousness, but merely true enough:

*Poetic Influence—when it involves two strong, authen-
tic poets,—always proceeds by a misreading of the prior
poet, an act of creative correction that is actually and nec-
essarily a misinterpretation. The history of fruitful poetic
influence, which is to say the main tradition of Western
poetry since the Renaissance, is a history of anxiety and
self-saving caricature, of distortion, of perverse, wilful re-
visionism without which modern poetry as such could not
exist.*

My own Idiot Questioner, happily curled up in the lab-
yrinth of my own being, protests: "What is the use of such
a principle, whether the argument it informs be true or
not?" Is it useful to be told that poets are not common
readers, and particularly are not critics, in the true sense

of critics, common readers raised to the highest power? And what *is* Poetic Influence anyway? Can the study of it really be anything more than the wearisome industry of source-hunting, of allusion-counting, an industry that will soon touch apocalypse anyway when it passes from scholars to computers? Is there not the shibboleth bequeathed us by Eliot, that the good poet steals, while the poor poet betrays an influence, borrows a voice? And are there not all the great Idealists of literary criticism, the deniers of poetic influence, ranging from Emerson with his maxims: "Insist on yourself: never imitate" and "Not possibly will the soul deign to repeat itself" to the recent transformation of Northrop Frye into the Arnold of our day, with his insistence that the Myth of Concern prevents poets from suffering the anxieties of obligation?

Against such idealism one cheerfully cites Lichtenberg's grand remark: "Yes, I too like to admire great men, but only those whose works I do not understand." Or again from Lichtenberg, who is one of the sages of Poetic Influence: "To do just the opposite is also a form of imitation, and the definition of imitation ought by rights to include both." What Lichtenberg implies is that Poetic Influence is itself an oxymoron, and he is right. But then, so is Romantic Love an oxymoron, and Romantic Love is the closest analogue of Poetic Influence, another splendid perversity of the spirit, though it moves precisely in the opposite direction. The poet confronting his Great Original must find the fault that is not there, and at the heart of all but the highest imaginative virtue. The lover is beguiled to the heart of loss, but is found, as he finds, within mutual illusion, the poem that is not there. "When two people fall in love," says Kierkegaard, "and begin to feel that they are made for one another, then it is time for them to break off, for by going on they have everything to lose and nothing to gain." When the ephebe, or figure of the youth as virile poet, is found by his Great Original, then it is time to go on, for he has everything to gain, and his precursor nothing to lose; if the fully written poets are indeed beyond loss.

But there is the state called Satan, and in that hardness poets must appropriate for themselves. For Satan is a pure or absolute consciousness of self compelled to have admitted its intimate alliance with opacity. The state of Satan is therefore a constant consciousness of dualism, of being trapped in the finite, not just in space (in the body) but in clock-time as well. To be pure spirit, yet to know in oneself the limit of opacity; to assert that one goes back before the Creation-Fall, yet be forced to yield to number, weight, and measure; this is the situation of the strong poet, the capable imagination, when he confronts the universe of poetry, the words that were and will be, the terrible splendor of cultural heritage. In our time, the situation becomes more desperate even than it was in the Milton-haunted eighteenth century, or the Wordsworth-haunted nineteenth, and our current and future poets have only the consolation that no certain Titanic figure has risen since Milton and Wordsworth, not even Yeats or Stevens.

If one examines the dozen or so major poetic influencers before this century, one discovers quickly who among them ranks as the great Inhibitor, the Sphinx who strangles even strong imaginations in their cradles: Milton. The motto to English poetry since Milton was stated by Keats: "Life to him would be Death to me." This deathly vitality in Milton is the state of Satan in him, and is shown us not so much by the character of Satan in *Paradise Lost* as by Milton's editorializing relationship to his own Satan, and by his relationship to all the stronger poets of the eighteenth century and to most of those in the nineteenth.

Milton is the central problem in any theory and history of poetic influence in English; perhaps more so even than Wordsworth, who is closer to us as he was to Keats, and who confronts us with everything that is most problematic in modern poetry, which is to say in ourselves. What unites this ruminative line—of which Milton is the ancestor; Wordsworth the great revisionist; Keats and Wallace Stevens, among others, the dependent heirs—is an honest acceptance of an actual dualism as opposed to the fierce desire to overcome all dualisms, a desire that dominates the visionary and prophetic line from the relative mildness of Spenser's temperament down through the various fiercenesses of Blake, Shelley, Browning, Whitman, and Yeats.

This is the authentic voice of the ruminative line, the poetry of loss, and the voice also of the strong poet accepting his task, rallying what remains:

> Farewell happy fields
> Where joy for ever dwells: Hail horrors, hail
> Infernal world, and thou profoundest Hell
> Receive thy new Possessor: One who brings
> A mind not to be chang'd by Place or Time,
> The mind is its own place, and in it self
> Can make a Heav'n of Hell, a Hell of Heav'n,
> What matter where, if I be still the same . . . ?

These lines, to the C. S. Lewis or Angelic School, represent moral idiocy, and are to be met with laughter, if we have remembered to start the day with our Good Morning's Hatred of Satan. If, however, we are not so morally sophisticated, we are likely to be very much moved by these lines. Not that Satan is not mistaken; of course he is. There is terrible pathos in his "if I be still the same," since he is not the same, and never will be again. But he knows it. He is adopting an heroic dualism, in this con-

scious farewell to Joy, a dualism upon which almost all
post-Miltonic poetic influence in the language founds it-
self.

To Milton, all fallen experience had its inevitable foun-
dation in loss, and paradise could be regained only by
One Greater Man, and not by any poet whatsoever. Yet
Milton's own Great Original, as he confessed to Dryden,
was Spenser, who allows his Colin a Poet's Paradise in
Book VI of *The Faerie Queene*. Milton—as both Johnson
and Hazlitt emphasize—was incapable of suffering the
anxiety of influence, unlike all of his descendants. John-
son insisted that, of all the borrowers from Homer, Mil-
ton was the least indebted, adding: "He was naturally a
thinker for himself, confident of his own abilities, and dis-
dainful of help or hindrance: he did not refuse admission
to the thought or images of his predecessors, but he did
not seek them." Hazlitt, in a lecture heard by Keats—an
influence upon Keats's subsequent notion of Negative
Capability—remarked upon Milton's positive capability
for ingesting his precursors: "In reading his works, we feel
ourselves under the influence of a mighty intellect, that
the nearer it approaches to others, becomes more distinct
from them." What then, we are compelled to inquire, did
Milton mean by nominating Spenser as his Great Original?
At least this: that in his Second Birth, Milton was re-born
into Spenser's romance world, and also that when he re-
placed what he came to regard as the unitary illusion of
Spenserian romance by an acceptance of an actual dualism
as the pain of being, he retained his sense of Spenser as
the sense of the Other, the dream of Otherness that all
poets must dream. In departing from the unitary aspi-
ration of his own youth Milton may be said to have fa-
thered the poetry that we call post-Enlightenment or Ro-
mantic, the poetry that takes as its obsessive theme the
power of the mind over the universe of death, or as Words-

worth phrased it, to what extent the mind is lord and master, outward sense the servant of her will.

No modern poet is unitary, whatever his stated beliefs. Modern poets are necessarily miserable dualists, because this misery, this poverty is the starting point of their art —Stevens speaks appropriately of the "profound poetry of the poor and of the dead." Poetry may or may not work out its own salvation in a man, but it comes only to those in dire imaginative need of it, though it may come then as terror. And this need is learned first through the young poet's or ephebe's experience of another poet, of the Other whose baleful greatness is enhanced by the ephebe's seeing him as a burning brightness against a framing darkness, rather as Blake's Bard of Experience sees the Tyger, or Job the Leviathan and Behemoth, or Ahab the White Whale or Ezekiel the Covering Cherub, for all these are visions of the Creation gone malevolent and entrapping, of a splendor menacing the Promethean Quester every ephebe is about to become.

For Collins, for Cowper, for many a Bard of Sensibility, Milton was the Tyger, the Covering Cherub blocking a new voice from entering the Poet's Paradise. The emblem of this discussion is the Covering Cherub. In Genesis he is God's Angel; in Ezekiel he is the Prince of Tyre; in Blake he is fallen Tharmas, and the Spectre of Milton; in Yeats he is the Spectre of Blake. In this discussion he is a poor demon of many names (as many names as there are strong poets) but I summon him first namelessly, as a final name is not yet devised by men for the anxiety that blocks their creativeness. He is that something that makes men victims and not poets, a demon of discursiveness and shady continuities, a pseudo-exegete who makes writings into Scriptures. He cannot strangle the imagination, for nothing can do that, and he in any case is too weak to strangle anything. The Covering Cherub may masquerade as the

Sphinx (as the Spectre of Milton masqueraded, in the nightmares of Sensibility) but the Sphinx (whose works are mighty) must be a female (or at least a female male). The Cherub is male (or at least a male female). The Sphinx riddles and strangles and is self-shattered at last, but the Cherub only covers, he only appears to block the way, he cannot do more than conceal. But the Sphinx *is* in the way, and must be dislodged. The unriddler is in every strong poet when he sets out upon his quest. It is the high irony of poetic vocation that the strong poets can accomplish the greater yet fail the lesser task. They push aside the Sphinx (else they could not be poets, not for more than one volume), but they cannot uncover the Cherub. More ordinary men (and sometimes weaker poets) can uncover enough of the Cherub so as to live (if not quite to choose Perfection of the Life), but approach the Sphinx only at the risk of death by throttling.

For the Sphinx is natural, but the Cherub is closer to the human. The Sphinx is sexual anxiety, but the Cherub is creative anxiety. The Sphinx is met upon the road back to origins, but the Cherub upon the road forward to possibility, if not to fulfillment. Good poets are powerful striders upon the way back—hence their profound joy as elegists—but only a few have opened themselves to vision. Uncovering the Cherub does not require power so much as it does persistence, remorselessness, constant wakefulness; for the blocking agent who obstructs creativity does not lapse into "stony sleep" as readily as the Sphinx does. Emerson thought that the poet unriddled the Sphinx by perceiving an identity in nature, or else yielded to the Sphinx, if he was merely bombarded by diverse particulars he could never hope to integrate. The Sphinx, as Emerson saw, is nature and the riddle of our emergence from nature, which is to say that the Sphinx is what psychoanalysts have called the Primal Scene. But what is the

Primal Scene, for a poet *as poet?* It is his Poetic Father's coitus with the Muse. There he was begotten? No—there they failed to beget him. He must be self-begotten, he must engender himself upon the Muse his mother. But the Muse is as pernicious as Sphinx or Covering Cherub, and may identify herself with either, though more usually with the Sphinx. The strong poet fails to beget himself— he must wait for his Son, who will define him even as he has defined his own Poetic Father. To beget here means to usurp, and is the dialectical labor of the Cherub. Entering here into the center of our sorrow, we must look clearly at him.

What does the Cherub cover, in Genesis? in Ezekiel? in Blake? Genesis 3:24—"So He drove out the man; and He placed at the east of the Garden of Eden the cherubim, and the flaming sword which turned every which way, to keep the way to the tree of life." The rabbis took the cherubim here to symbolize the terror of God's *presence;* to Rashi they were "Angels of destruction." Ezekiel 28:14–16 gives us an even fiercer text:

> Thou wast the far-covering [*mimshach,* "far-extending," according to Rashi] cherub; and I set thee, so that thou wast upon the holy mountain of God; thou hast walked up and down in the midst of the stones of the fire. Thou wast perfect in thy ways from the day that thou wast created, till unrighteousness was found in thee. By the multitude of thy traffic they filled the midst of thee with violence, and thou hast sinned; therefore have I cast thee as profane out of the mountain of God; and I will destroy you, O Covering Cherub, in the midst of the stones of the fire.

Here God denounces the Prince of Tyre, who is a cherub because the cherubim in the tabernacle and in Solomon's Temple spread their wings over the ark, and so protected it, even as the Prince of Tyre once protected Eden, the garden of God. Blake is a still fiercer prophet against the Covering Cherub. To Blake, Voltaire and Rousseau were Vala's Covering Cherubim, Vala being the illusory beauty of the natural world, and the prophets of naturalistic enlightenment being her servitors. In Blake's "brief epic," called *Milton,* the Covering Cherub stands between the achieved Man who is at once Milton, Blake, and Los, and the emanation or beloved. In Blake's *Jerusalem* the Cherub stands as blocking agent between Blake-Los and Jesus. The answer to what the Cherub covers is therefore: in Blake, everything that nature itself covers; in Ezekiel, the richness of the earth, but by the Blakean paradox of *appearing to be those riches;* in Genesis, the Eastern Gate, the Way to the Tree of Life.

The Covering Cherub separates, then? No—he has no power to do so. Poetic Influence is not a separation but a victimization—it is a destruction of desire. The emblem of Poetic Influence is the Covering Cherub because the Cherub symbolizes what came to be the Cartesian category of *extensiveness;* hence it is described as *mimshach*—"far-extending." It is not accidental that Descartes and his fellows and disciples are the ultimate enemies of poetic vision in the Romantic tradition, for the Cartesian *extensiveness* is the root category of modern (as opposed to Pauline) dualism, of the dumbfoundering abyss between ourselves and the object. Descartes saw objects as localized space; the irony of Romantic vision is that it rebelled against Descartes, but except in Blake did not go far enough— Wordsworth and Freud alike remain Cartesian dualists, for whom the present is a precipitated past, and nature a continuum of localized spaces. These Cartesian reductions of time and space brought upon us the further blight of the negative aspect of poetic influence, of *influenza* in the realm of literature, as the influx of an epidemic of anxiety. Instead of the radiation of an aetherial fluid we received the poetic flowing in of an occult power exercised by humans, rather than by stars upon humans; "occult" because invisible and insensible. Cut mind as *intensiveness* off from the outer world as *extensiveness,* and mind will learn—as never before—its own solitude. The solitary brooder moves to deny his sonship and his brotherhood, even as Blake's Urizen, a satire upon Cartesian *Genius,* is the archetype of the strong poet afflicted by the anxiety of influence. If there are two, disjunctive worlds —one a huge mathematical machine extended in space, and the other made up of unextended, thinking spirits —then we will start locating our anxieties back along that continuum extended into the past, and our vision of the Other will become magnified when the Other is placed in the past.

The Covering Cherub then is a demon of continuity; his baleful charm imprisons the present in the past, and reduces a world of differences into a grayness of uniformity. The identity of past and present is at one with the essential identity of all objects. This is Milton's "universe of death" and with it poetry cannot live, for poetry must leap, it must locate itself in a discontinuous universe, and it must make that universe (as Blake did) if it cannot find one. Discontinuity is freedom. Prophets and advanced analysts alike proclaim discontinuity; here Shelley and the phenomenologists are in agreement: "To predict, to really foretell, is still a gift of those who own the future in the full unrestricted sense of the word, the sense of what is coming toward us, and not of what is the result of the past." That is J. H. Van den Berg in his *Metabletica.* In Shelley's *A Defence of Poetry,* which Yeats rightly considered the most profound discourse upon poetry in the language, the prophetic voice trumpets the same freedom:

"Poets are the hierophants of an unapprehended inspiration; the mirrors of the gigantic shadows which futurity casts upon the present."

"He proves God by exhaustion" is Samuel Beckett's own note on "So I'm not my son" in his poem *Whoroscope,* a dramatic monologue spoken by Descartes. The triumph of Descartes came in a literal vision, not necessarily friendly to imaginations other than his own. The protests against Cartesian reductiveness never cease, in constant involuntary tribute to him. Beckett's fine handful of poems in English are too subtle to protest overtly, but they are strong prayers for discontinuity.

Yet there is no overt Cartesian prejudice against poets, no analogue to the Platonic polemic against their authority. Descartes, in his *Private Thoughts,* could even write: "It might seem strange that opinions of weight are found in the works of poets rather than philosophers. The reason is that poets wrote through enthusiasm and imagination; there are in us seeds of knowledge, as of fire in a flint; philosophers extract them by way of reason, but poets strike them out by imagination, and then they shine more bright." The Cartesian myth or abyss of consciousness nevertheless took the fire from the flint, and trapped poets in what Blake grimly called a "cloven fiction," with the alternatives, both anti-poetic, of Idealism and Materialism. Philosophy, in cleansing itself, has rinsed away this great dualism, but the whole of the giant line from Milton down to Yeats and Stevens had only their own tradition, Poetic Influence, to tell them that "both Idealism and Materialism are answers to an improper question." Yeats and Stevens, as much as Descartes (or Wordsworth), labored to see with the mind and not with the bodily eye alone; Blake, the one genuine anti-Cartesian, found such labor too a cloven fiction, and satirized the Cartesian Dioptrics by opposing his Vortex to that of the Mechanist.

That the Mechanism had its desperate nobility we grant now; Descartes wished to save the phenomena by his myth of *extensiveness*. A body took definite shape, moved within a fixed area, and was divided within that area; and thus maintained an integrity in its strictly limited becoming. This established the world or manifold of sensation *given* to the poets, and from it the Wordsworthian vision could begin, rising from this confinement to the enforced ecstasy of the further reduction Wordsworth chose to call Imagination. The manifold of sensation in *Tintern Abbey* initially is further isolated, and then dissolved into a fluid continuum, with the edges of things, the fixities and definites, fading out into a "higher" apprehension. Blake's protest against Wordsworthianism, the more effective for its praise of Wordsworth's poetry, is founded on his horror of this enforced illusion, this ecstasy that is a reduction. In the Cartesian theory of vortices all motion had to be circular (there being no vacuum for matter to move through) and all matter had to be capable of further reduction (there were thus no atoms). These, to Blake, were the circlings of the Mills of Satan, grinding on vainly in their impossible task of reducing the Minute Particulars, the Atoms of Vision that will not further divide. In the Blakean theory of vortices, circular motion is a self-contradiction; when the poet stands at the apex of his own Vortex the Cartesian-Newtonian circles resolve into the flat plain of Vision, and the Particulars stand forth, each as itself, and not another thing. For Blake does not wish to save the phenomena, any more than he joins the long program of those who seek "to save the appearances," in the sense that Owen Barfield (taking the phrase from Milton) has traced. Blake is the theorist of the saving or revisionary aspect of Poetic Influence, of the impulse that attempts to cast out the Covering Cherub into the midst of the stones of the fire.

French visionaries, because so close to the spell of Descartes, to the Cartesian Siren, have worked in a different spirit, in the high and serious humor, the apocalyptic irony, that culminates in the work of Jarry and his disciples. The study of Poetic Influence is necessarily a branch of 'Pataphysics, and gladly confesses its indebtedness to ". . . *the* Science, of Imaginary Solutions." As Blake's Los, under the influence of Urizen, the master Cartesian, comes crashing down in our Creation-Fall, he *swerves,* and this parody of the Lucretian *clinamen,* this change from destiny to slight caprice, is, with final irony, *all* the individuality of Urizenic creation, of Cartesian vision as such. The *clinamen* or swerve, which is the Urizenic equivalent of the hapless errors of re-creation made by the Platonic demiurge, is necessarily the central working concept of the theory of Poetic Influence, for what divides each poet from his Poetic Father (and so saves, by division) is an instance of creative revisionism. We must understand that the *clinamen* stems always from a 'Pataphysical sense of the arbitrary. The poet so stations his precursor, so swerves his context, that the visionary objects, with their higher intensity, fade into the continuum. The poet has, in regard to the precursor's heterocosm, a shuddering sense of the arbitrary—of the equality, or equal haphazardness, of all objects. This sense is *not reductive,* for it is the continuum, the stationing context, that is reseen, and shaped into the visionary; it is brought up to the intensity of the crucial objects, which then "fade" into it, in a manner opposite to the Wordsworthian "fade into the light of common day." 'Pataphysics proves to be truly accurate; in the world of poets all regularities are indeed "regular exceptions"; the *recurrence* of vision is itself a law governing exceptions. If every act of vision determines a particular law, then the basis for the splendidly horrible paradox of Poetic Influence is securely founded; the new poet *himself* determines the precursor's *particular* law. If a creative interpretation is thus necessarily a misinterpretation, we must accept this apparent absurdity. It is absurdity of the highest mode, the apocalyptic absurdity of Jarry, or of Blake's entire enterprise.

Let us make then the dialectical leap: most so-called "accurate" interpretations of poetry are worse than mistakes; perhaps there are only more or less creative or interesting mis-readings, for is not every reading necessarily a *clinamen?* Should we not therefore, in this spirit, attempt to renew the study of poetry by returning yet again to fundamentals? No poem has sources, and no poem merely alludes to another. Poems are written by men, and not by anonymous Splendors. The stronger the man, the larger his resentments, and the more brazen his *clinamen*. But at what price, as readers, are we to forfeit our own *clinamen?*

I propose, not another new poetics, but a wholly different practical criticism. Let us give up the failed enterprise of seeking to "understand" any single poem as an entity in itself. Let us pursue instead the quest of learning to read any poem as its poet's deliberate misinterpretation, *as a poet,* of a precursor poem or of poetry in general. Know each poem by its *clinamen* and you will "know" that poem in a way that will not purchase knowledge by the loss of the poem's power. I say this in the spirit of Pater's rejection of Coleridge's famous organic analogue. Pater felt that Coleridge (however involuntarily) slighted the poet's pain and suffering in achieving his poem, sorrows at least partly dependent upon the anxiety of influence, and sorrows not separate from the poem's meaning.

Borges, commenting on Pascal's sublime and terrifying sense of his Fearful Sphere, contrasts Pascal to Bruno, who in 1584 could still react with exultation to the Copernican Revolution. In seventy years, senescence sets in—Donne, Milton, Glanvill see decay where Bruno saw only

joy in the advance of thought. As Borges sums it, "In that
dispirited century, the absolute space which had inspired
the hexameters of Lucretius, the absolute space which had
meant liberation to Bruno, became a labyrinth and an
abyss for Pascal." Borges does not lament the change, for
Pascal too achieves the Sublime. But strong *poets,* unlike
Pascal, do not exist to accept griefs; they cannot rest with
purchasing the Sublime at so high a price. Like Lucretius
himself, they opt for *clinamen* as freedom. Here is Lucre-
tius:

> When the atoms are travelling straight down through
> empty space by their own weight, at quite indeterminate
> times and places they *swerve* ever so little from their
> course, just so much that you can call it a change of direction.
> If it were not for this swerve, everything would fall down-
> wards like rain-drops through the abyss of space. No col-
> lision would take place and no impact of atom on atom
> would be created. Thus nature would never have created any-
> thing. . . .
> But the fact that the mind itself has no internal necessity
> to determine its every act and compel it to suffer in helpless
> passivity—this is due to the slight swerve of the atoms at no
> determinate time or place.

Contemplating the *clinamen* of Lucretius, we can see
the final irony of Poetic Influence, and come full circle to
end where we began. This *clinamen* between the strong
poet and the Poetic Father is made by the whole being of
the later poet, and the true history of modern poetry
would be the accurate recording of these revisionary
swerves. To the pure 'Pataphysician, the swerve is marvel-
ously gratuitous; Jarry, after all, was capable of consider-
ing the Passion as an uphill bicycle race. The student of
Poetic Influence is compelled to be an impure 'Pataphysi-
cian; he must understand that the *clinamen* always must

be considered as though it were simultaneously intentional and involuntary, the Spiritual Form of each poet *and* the gratuitous gesture each poet makes as his falling body hits the floor of the abyss. Poetic Influence is the passing of Individuals through States, in Blake's language, but the passing is done ill when it is not a swerving. The strong poet indeed says: "I seem to have stopped falling; now I *am fallen,* consequently, I lie here in Hell," but he is thinking, as he says this, "As I fell, *I swerved,* consequently I lie here in a Hell improved by my own making."

Two

In every work of genius we recognize our own rejected thoughts —they come back to us with a certain alienated majesty.

EMERSON

Tessera

or COMPLETION
AND ANTITHESIS

I first read Nietzsche's essay *Of the Advantage and Disadvantage of History for Life* in October 1951, when I was a graduate student at Yale. The essay was chastening then, and hurts more when I read it now:

> The most astonishing works may be created; the swarm of historical neuters will always be in their place, ready to consider the author through their long telescopes. The echo is heard at once, but always in the form of "criticism," though the critic never dreamed of the work's possibility a moment before. It never comes to have an influence, but only a criticism; and the criticism itself has no influence, but only breeds another criticism. And so we come to consider the fact of many critics as a mark of failure. Actually everything remains in the old condition, even in the presence of such "influence": men talk a little while of a new thing, and then of some other new thing, and in the meantime they do what they have always done. The historical training of our critics prevents their having an influence in the true sense—an influence on life and action.

It never needs a Nietzsche to scorn criticism, and the scorn in this passage did not trouble me when first I read it, nor does it trouble me now. But its implicit definition of critical "influence" must be a burden for critics always. Nietzsche, like Emerson, is one of the great deniers of anxiety-as-influence, just as Johnson and Coleridge are among its great affirmers, and as W. J. Bate (following Johnson and Coleridge) is its most considerable recent scholar. Yet I find my own understanding of the anxiety of influence owes more to Nietzsche and Emerson, who apparently did not feel it, than to Johnson, Coleridge, and their admirable scholar, Bate. Nietzsche, as he always insisted, was the heir of Goethe in his strangely optimistic refusal to regard the poetical past as primarily an obstacle to fresh creation. Goethe, like Milton, absorbed precursors with a gusto evidently precluding anxiety. Nietzsche owed as much to Goethe and to Schopenhauer as Emerson did to Wordsworth and Coleridge, but Nietzsche, like Emerson, did not feel the chill of being darkened by a precursor's shadow. "Influence," to Nietzsche, meant vitalization. But influence, and more precisely poetic influence, has been more of a blight than a blessing, from the Enlightenment until this moment. Where it has vitalized, it has operated as misprision, as deliberate, even perverse revisionism.

Nietzsche, in his *Twilight of the Idols,* states his conception of genius:

> Great men, like great ages, are explosives in which a tremendous force is stored up; their precondition is always, historically and physiologically, that for a long time much has been gathered, stored up, saved up, and conserved for them —that there has been no explosion for a long time. Once the tension in the mass has become too great, then the most accidental stimulus suffices to summon into the world the "genius," the "deed," the great destiny. What does the environment matter then, or the age, or the "spirit of the age," or "public opinion."

The genius is *strong,* his age is *weak.* And his strength exhausts, not himself, but those who come in his wake. He *floods* them, and in return, Nietzsche insists, they misunderstand their benefactor (though from Nietzsche's description I am tempted to say, not their benefactor but their calamity).

Goethe, who may be termed Nietzsche's grandfather even as Schopenhauer was his father, remarks in his *Theory of Color* that "even perfect models have a disturbing effect in that they lead us to skip necessary stages in our *Bildung,* with the result, for the most part, that we are carried wide of the mark into limitless error." Yet elsewhere Goethe states the conviction that models are only mirrors for the self anyway: "To be loved for what one is, is the greatest exception. The great majority love in another only what they lend him, their own selves, their version of him." We need to remember that Goethe believed in what he called, with charming irony, recurrent puberty, or as he blandly said: "The individual has to be ruined again." How often? we sometimes want to ask, troubled also by the Goethean insistence upon being influenced by every possible engulfment: "Everything great molds us from the moment we become aware of it." This formula is terrible in its consequences for most poets (and for most men). But Goethe, in his autobiography, was capable of a passage like the following, which only Milton among the post-Enlightenment English, and only Emerson among Americans, might have been tempted to endorse. Only a poet who believed himself literally incapable of creative anxiety could say this:

To be sure, it is a tedious and at times melancholy business, this overconcentration on ourselves and what harms and helps us. But considering the ominous idiosyncrasy of human nature on the one hand and the infinite diversity of modes of life and enjoyments on the other, it is a sheer miracle that the human race has not long since wrought its own destruction. It must be that human nature is endowed with a peculiar tenacity and versatility enabling it to overcome everything that it contacts or takes into itself, or, if the thing defies assimilation, at least to render it innocuous.

This is truer of Goethean than of human nature. "Every talent must unfold itself in fighting," Nietzsche remarks, and so his vision of Goethe is of a fighter for *Totality,* against even the formulations of Kant. To Nietzsche though, Goethe is at last another overcoming of the merely human: "he disciplined himself to wholeness, he *created* himself." What are we to make of such an assertion? First, that it is soundly based on Goethe's own appalling self-confidence. Is he not recorded as having said: "Do not all the achievements of a poet's predecessors and contemporaries rightfully belong to him? Why should he shrink from picking flowers where he finds them? Only by making the riches of the others our own do we bring anything great into being." Or, still more forcefully, to Eckermann he said: "There is all this talk about originality, but what does it amount to? As soon as we are born the world begins to influence us, and this goes on till we die. And anyway, what can we in fact call our own except the energy, the force, the will!" Except not less than everything, for a poet, I am compelled to murmur as I read this, for what does the anxiety of influence concern but the energy, the force, the will? Are they one's own, or emanations from the other, from the precursor? Thomas Mann, a great sufferer from the anxiety of influence, and one of the great theorists of that anxiety, suffered more acutely for Goethe's not having suffered at all, as Mann realized. Questing for some sign of such anxiety in Goethe, he came up with a single question from the *Westöstlicher Diwan:* "Does a man live when others also live?" The question troubled Mann far more than it did Goethe. The talkative musical promoter in *Dr. Faustus,* Herr Saul Fitelberg, utters a central obsession of the novel when he observes to Leverkühn: "You insist on the incomparableness of the personal case. You pay tribute to an arrogant personal uniqueness—maybe you have to do that. 'Does one live when others live?' " In his book on the genesis of *Dr. Faustus,* Mann admits to his anxiety on receiving the *Glasperlenspiel* of Hesse while at work composing his intended late masterpiece. In his diary, he wrote: "To be reminded that one is not alone in the world—always unpleasant," and then he added: "It is another version of Goethe's question: 'Do we then live if others live?' " A reader may smile at the vanity of greatness and perhaps murmur: "We charmers do not love one another," but the matter is, alas, profound, as Mann well knew. In his powerful essay on *Freud and the Future,* Mann comes very close to Nietzsche's dark essay on the right use of history (which Mann later re-read for use in *Faustus*). "The ego of antiquity and its consciousness of itself," Mann says, "were different from our own, less exclusive, less sharply defined." Life could be "imitation," in the sense of mythical identification, and could find "self-awareness, sanction, consecration" in such renewal of an earlier identity. Following (as he thought) Freud, while invoking the exemplary life of Goethe, and hinting at his own pattern of the *imitatio* Goethe, Mann gives us a twentieth-century version of Nietzsche's overcoming of the anxiety of influence. I quote all of this passage in Mann's essay, as it seems to me unique in our century's attitudes towards the sorrows of influence:

Infantilism—in other words, regression to childhood— what a role this genuinely psychoanalytic element plays in all our lives! What a large share it has in shaping the life of a human being; operating, indeed, in just the way I have described: as mythical identification, as survival, as a treading in footprints already made! The bond with the father, the imitation of the father, the game of being the father, and the transference to father-substitute pictures of a higher and more developed type—how these infantile traits work upon the life of the individual to mark and shape it! I use the word "shape," for to me in all seriousness the happiest, most pleasurable element of what we call education (*Bildung*), the shaping of the human being, is just this powerful influence of admiration and love, this childish identification with a father-image elected out of profound affinity. The artist in particular, a passionately childlike and play-possessed being, can tell us of the mysterious yet after all obvious effect of such infantile imitation upon his own life, his productive conduct of a career which after all is often nothing but a reanimation of the hero under very different temporal and personal conditions and with very different, shall we say childish means. The *imitatio* Goethe, with its Werther and Wilhelm Meister stages, its old-age period of *Faust* and *Diwan,* can still shape and mythically mould the life of an artist—rising out of his unconscious, yet playing over—as is the artist way—into a smiling, childlike, and profound awareness.

Everything of the relation between ephebe and precursor that matters is in this passage, with the exception of what matters most—the inescapable melancholy, the anxiety that makes misprision inevitable. Mann's swerve away from Goethe is the profoundly ironic denial that any swerve is necessary. His misinterpretation of Goethe is to read precisely his own parodistic genius, his own kind of loving irony, into his precursor. In his great effort at portraying *Bildung,* his Joseph-Saga, he gives us the memorable figure of Tamar, who loves Judah for the sake of an idea, and murders his sons with her loins in her quest after that idea. "It was," Mann writes, "a new basis for love, for the first time in existence: love which comes not from the flesh but from the idea, so that one might well call it daemonic." Tamar comes late in the story, but is very sure of the central place in the story that she will compel the story to make for her. She stands, as Mann perhaps only partly realized (great ironist though he was) in some sense for Mann himself, and for any artist who feels strongly the injustice of time, at having denied him all priority. Mann's Tamar knows instinctively that the meaning of one copulation is only another copulation, even as Mann knows that one cannot write a novel without remembering another novel. "Forgetfulness," Nietzsche had insisted, "is a property of all action," and he went on to quote Goethe's phrase that the man of action is without conscience. So, Nietzsche could add, the man of action, the true poet, "is also without knowledge: he forgets most things in order to do one, he is unjust to what is behind him, and only recognizes one law—the law of that which is to be." Nothing—I must insist—could be more nobly and self-deceptively false than Nietzsche's insistence, the insistence of a poet who is desperately afraid of irony. This irony emerges in a pungent and terrible passage in the essay on history, where Nietzsche most powerfully protests the Hegelian philosophy of history:

> The belief that one is a late-comer in the world is, anyhow, harmful and degrading; but it must appear frightful and devastating when it raises our late-comer to godhead, by a neat turn of the wheel, as the true meaning and object of all past creation, and his conscious misery is set up as the perfection of the world's history.

Never mind that this irony is directed against Hegel; its true object is the anxiety of influence within Nietzsche himself. "I am convinced," Lichtenberg wisely tells us, "that a person doesn't only love himself in others, he also hates himself in others." The great deniers of influence—Goethe, Nietzsche, Mann in Germany; Emerson and Thoreau in America; Blake and Lawrence in England; Pascal and Rousseau and Hugo in France—these central men are enormous fields of the anxiety of influence, as much so as its great affirmers, from Samuel Johnson through Coleridge and Ruskin in England, and the strong poets of the last several generations in all four countries.

Montaigne asks us to search within ourselves, to learn there "that our private wishes are for the most part born and nourished at the expense of others." Montaigne more even than Johnson is the great realist of the anxiety of influence, at least until Freud. Montaigne tells us (following Aristotle) that Homer was both the first and last of poets. Sometimes in reading Pascal, one feels that he feared Montaigne to have been the first and last of true moralists. Pascal huffed: "It is not in Montaigne, but in myself, that I find all that I see in him," an assertion that becomes funny when we consult a good edition of Pascal, and study the immense lists of "parallel passages" that demonstrate an indebtedness so pervasive as to be a scandal. Pascal attempting to refute Montaigne while wearing his precursor's coat is rather like Matthew Arnold sneering at Keats while writing *The Scholar Gipsy* and *Thyrsis* in a diction, tone, and sensuous rhythm wholly (and unconsciously) stolen from the Great Odes.

Kierkegaard, in *Fear and Trembling,* announces, with magnificent but absurdly apocalyptic confidence, that he who is willing to work gives birth to his own father." I find truer to mere fact the aphoristic admission of Nietzsche: "When one hasn't had a good father, it is necessary to invent one." I am afraid that the anxiety of influence, from which we all suffer, whether we are poets or not, has to be located first in its origins, in the fateful morasses of what Freud, with grandly desperate wit, called "the family romance." But, before entering on that balefully enchanted ground, I pause at "anxiety" itself, for some needful recognitions.

Freud, in defining anxiety, speaks of "angst vor etwas." Anxiety *before* something is clearly a mode of expectation, like desire. We can say that anxiety and desire are the antinomies of the ephebe or beginning poet. The anxiety of influence is an anxiety in expectation of *being flooded*. Lacan insists that desire is only a metonymy, and it may be that desire's contrary, the anxiety of expectation, is only a metonymy also. The ephebe who fears his precursors as he might fear a flood is taking a vital part for a whole, the whole being everything that constitutes his creative anxiety, the spectral blocking agent in every poet. Yet this metonymy is hardly to be avoided; every good reader properly *desires* to drown, but if the poet drowns, he will become *only a reader*.

We live increasingly in a time where soft-headed descriptions of anxiety are marketable, and cheerfully consumed. Only one analysis of anxiety in this century adds anything of value, in my judgment, to the legacy of the classical moralists and Romantic speculators and necessarily that contribution is Freud's. First, he reminds us, anxiety is something felt, but it is a state of unpleasure different from sorrow, grief, and mere mental tension. Anxiety, he says, is unpleasure accompanied by efferent or discharge phenomena among definite pathways. These discharge phenomena relieve the "increase of excitation" that underlies anxiety. The primal increase of excitation may be the birth trauma, itself a response to our first situation of *danger*. Freud's use of "danger" reminds us of our universal fear of domination, of our being trapped by nature in our body as a dungeon, in certain situations of stress. Though Freud rejected Rank's account of the birth trauma as being biologically unfounded, he remained troubled by what he called "a certain predisposition to anxiety on the part of the infant." Separation from the mother, analogous to later castration anxiety, brings on "an increase of tension arising from nongratification of needs," the "needs" here being vital to the economy of self-preservation. Separation anxiety is thus an anxiety of exclusion, and rapidly joins itself to death anxiety, or the ego's fear of superego. This brings Freud to the border of his definition of compulsion neuroses, which are due to dread of the superego, and encourages us to explore the compulsive analogue of the melancholy of poets, or the anxiety of influence.

When a poet experiences incarnation *qua* poet, he experiences anxiety necessarily towards any danger that might *end him* as a poet. The anxiety of influence is so terrible because it is both a kind of separation anxiety and the beginning of a compulsion neurosis, or fear of a death that is a personified superego. Poems, we can speculate analogically, may be viewed (humorously) as motor discharges in response to the excitation increase of influence anxiety. Poems, as criticism always has assured us, must give pleasure. But—despite the insistence of whole traditions of poetry and of Romanticism in particular—poems are not given *by* pleasure, but by the unpleasure of a dangerous situation, the situation of anxiety of which the grief of influence forms so large a part.

What justifies this radical analogue between human and poetic birth, between biological and creative anxiety? To give justification we need to tread on shadowy and daemonic ground, in the sorrow of origins, where art rises from shamanistic ecstasy and the squalor of our timeless human fear of mortality. Because my interests are those of the practical critic, seeking a newer and starker way of reading poems, I find this return to origins inescapable, though distasteful. What both holds rival poems together and yet keeps them apart is an antithetical relation that rises, in the first place, from the primordial element in poetry; and that element, sorrowfully, is divination, or the desperation of seeking to foretell dangers to the self, whether from nature, the gods, from others, or indeed from the very self. And—I must add—for the poet *in a poet*—these dangers come also from other poems.

There are many theories of poetic origins. Of these, I am most convinced yet also most repelled by Vico's, but the repulsion is due to my own addiction to a Romantic and prophetic humanism, and so I must set it aside. Yet Emerson, the great American fountainhead of a Romantic, prophetic humanism, is curiously Viconian also in his theorizings on poetic origins, which I accept as an encouragement. For Vico, as Auerbach observed, there is no knowledge without creation. Vico's primitive men are beautifully described by Auerbach as "originally solitary nomads living in orderless promiscuity within the chaos of a mysterious and for this very reason horrible nature. They had no faculties of reasoning; they only had very strong sensations and a strength of imagination such as civilized men can hardly understand." To govern their life, Vico's primitives created a system of ceremonial magic that was what Vico himself called "a severe poem." These primitives—giants of the imagination—were poets, and their ceremonial wisdom was what we still seek as "poetic wisdom." Yet—though this did not bother Vico —this wisdom, this magic formalism, was cruel and selfish, necessarily. The giant forms who invented poetry are the anthropological equivalents of wizards, medicine men, shamans, whose vocation is survival and teaching others to survive. Poetic wisdom—to Vico—is founded upon divination, and to sing is—simply and even etymologically— to foretell. Poetic thought is proleptic, and the Muse invoked under the name of Memory is being implored to help the poet remember the future. Shamans return to primordial chaos, in their terrible and total initiations, in order to make fresh creation possible; but in societies no longer primitive such returns are rare. Poets from the Greek Orphics to our contemporaries live in guilt cultures, where the magic formalism of Viconian poetic wisdom is necessarily unacceptable. Empedocles may be chronologically the last poet who meant his divination literally. That is, he believed he had made himself a god by being a brilliantly successful practitioner of augury. Compared to his blatancy, strong poets like Dante, Milton, and Goethe seem consumed by the anxiety of influence, miraculously free of it though they seem when we compare them to the major Romantics and Moderns.

Curtius, in his famous account of the Muses, sees them as a problem in historical devaluation or replacement, as well as in continuity, and finds their significance for even the Greeks to have been "vague." But Vico is very precise as to the Muses' significance for his concept of the Poetic Character:

Poets were properly called divine in the sense of diviners, from *divinari,* to divine or predict. Their science was called Muse, defined by Homer as the knowledge of good and evil, that is, divination. . . . The Muse must thus have been properly at first the science of divining by auspices. . . . Urania, whose name is from *ouranos,* heaven, and signifies "she who contemplates the heavens" to take thence the auspices. . . . She and the other Muses were held to be daughters of Jove (for religion gave birth to all the arts of humanity, of which Apollo, held to be principally the god of divination, is the presiding deity), and they "sing" in the sense in which the Latin verbs *camere* and *cantare* mean "foretell."

I submit that these sentences (I have run them together from several passages in Vico) have dark implications for any study of poets and poetry. Poetic anxiety implores the Muse for aid in divination, which means to foretell and put off as long as possible the poet's own death, as poet and (perhaps secondarily) as man. The poet of any guilt culture whatsoever cannot initiate himself into a fresh chaos; he is compelled to accept a lack of priority in creation, which means he must accept also a failure in divination, as the first of many little deaths that prophesy a final and total extinction. His word is not his own word only, and his Muse has whored with many before him. He has come late in the story, but she has always been central in it, and he rightly fears that his impending catastrophe is only another in her litany of sorrows. What is his sincerity to her? The longer he dwells with her, the smaller he becomes, as though he proved man only by exhaustion. The poet thinks he loves the Muse out of his longing for divination, which will guarantee him time enough for fulfillment, but his only longing is a homesickness for a house as large as his spirit, and so he doesn't love the Muse at all. Blake's *The Mental Traveller* shows us what the mutual love of poet and Muse actually is. Yet what does the poet's homesickness have in it that is valid? He errs in seeking imagoes—the Muse was never his mother nor the precursor his father. His mother was his imagined spirit or idea of his own sublimity, and his father will not be born until he himself finds his own central ephebe, who retrospectively will beget him upon the Muse, who at last and only then will become his mother. Illusion upon illusion, since the earth, as Keats's Muse Moneta assures him, is justified without all this suffering, this infliction of family romance upon the traditions of poetry. Yet the burden is still there. Nietzsche, the prophet of vitalism, who began by decrying the abuse of history, calls out: "But do I bid thee be either plant or phantom?" and every strong poet answers: "Yet I must be both."

Perhaps then we can reduce by saying that the young poet loves himself in the Muse, and fears that she hates herself in him. The ephebe cannot know that he is an invalid of Cartesian *extensiveness,* a young man in the horror of discovering his own incurable case of continuity. By the time he has become a strong poet, and so learned this dilemma, he seeks to exorcise the necessary guilt of his ingratitude by turning his precursor into a fouled version of the later poet himself. But that too is a self-deception and a banality, for what the strong poet thus does is to transform himself into a fouled version of himself, and then confound the consequence with the figure of the precursor.

Freud distinguishes between two late phases of the family romance, one in which the child believes himself to be a changeling, and one in which he believes his mother to have had many lovers in place of his father. The movement between fantasies here is suggestively reductive, as the notion of a higher origin and thwarted destiny yields to images of erotic degradation. Blake, by insisting that Tirzah or Necessity was mother only of his mortal part, found (as almost always) a dialectic of distinctions that liberated him from the concerns of the family romance. But most poets—like most men—suffer some version of the family romance as they struggle to define their most advantageous relation to their precursor and their Muse. The strong poet—like the Hegelian great man—is both hero of poetic history and victim of it. This victimization has increased as history proceeds because the anxiety of influence is strongest where poetry is most lyrical, most subjective, and stemming directly from the personality. In the Hegelian view a poem is only a prelude to a religious perception, and in an advanced lyrical poem the spirit is so separated from the sensuous that art is at the point of dissolving into religion. But no strong poet, in his quest-ing prime, can (as poet) accept this Hegelian view. And history is no consolation, to him of all men, for his victim-ization.

If he himself is not to be victimized, then the strong poet must "rescue" the beloved Muse from his precursors. Of course, he "overestimates" the Muse, seeing her as unique and irreplaceable, for how else can he be assured that *he* is unique and irreplaceable? Freud dryly remarks that "the pressing desire in the unconscious for some irre-placeable thing often resolves itself into an endless series in actuality," a pattern particularly prevalent in the love life of most poets, or perhaps of any post-Romantic men and women cursed with strong imagination. "A thing," Freud adds, "which in consciousness makes its appearance as two contraries is often in the unconscious a united whole," which is a remark we will need to go back to when we venture into the abyss of antithetical meanings. In the wholeness of the poet's imagination, the Muse is mother and harlot at once, for the largest phantasmagoria most of us weave from our necessarily egoistic interests is the family romance, which might be called the only poem that even unpoetical natures continue to compose. But to understand that the poet's difficult relation to precursor and to Muse is a more extreme version of this common malady, we need to recall Freud at his canniest. A rather long passage of his darkest wisdom must be cited:

When a child hears that he owes his life to his parents, that his mother gave him life, the feelings of tenderness in him mingle with the longing to be big and independent himself, so that he forms the wish to repay the parents for this gift and requite it by one of a like value. It is as though the boy said in his defiance: "I want nothing from father; I shall repay him all I have cost him." He then weaves a phantasy of saving his father's life on some dangerous occasion by which he becomes quits with him, and this phantasy is commonly enough displaced on to the Emperor, the King, or any other great man, after which it can enter consciousness and is even made use of by poets. So far as it applies to the father, the attitude of defiance in the "saving" phantasy far outweighs the tender feeling in it, the latter being usually directed towards the mother. The mother gave the child his life and it is not easy to replace this unique gift with anything of equal value. By a slight change of meaning, which is easily effected in the unconscious—comparable to the way in which shades of meaning merge into one another in conscious conceptions—rescuing the mother acquires the significance of giving her a child or making one for her—one like himself, of course . . . all the instincts, the loving, the grateful, the sensual, the defiant, the self-assertive and independent—all are gratified in the wish to be *the father of himself.*

If this is to serve as model for the family romance between poets, it needs to be transformed, so as to place the emphasis less upon phallic fatherhood, and more upon *priority,* for the commodity in which poets deal, their authority, their property, turns upon priority. They own, they are, what they become first in naming. Indeed, they all follow the intuition of Valéry, when he insisted that man fabricates by abstraction, a withdrawal that takes the made thing *out from* the cosmos and from time, so that it may be called one's own, a place where no trespass can be permitted. All quest-romances of the post-Enlightenment, meaning all Romanticisms whatsoever, are quests to re-beget one's own self, to become one's own Great Original. We journey to abstract ourselves by fabrication. But where the fabric already has been woven, we journey to unravel. Alas—in art—the quest is more illusory even than it is in life. Identity recedes from us in our lives the more we pursue it, yet we are right not to be persuaded that it is unattainable. Geoffrey Hartman notes that in a poem the identity quest always is something of a deception, because the quest always works as a formal device. This is part of the maker's agony, part of why influence is so deep an anxiety for the strong poet and compels him to an otherwise unnecessary inclination or bias in his work. No one can bear to see his own inner struggle as being mere artifice, yet the poet, in writing his poem, is forced to see the assertion against influence as being a ritualized quest for identity. Can the seducer say to his Muse: "Madam, my deception is imposed upon me by the formal demands of my art"?

Our sorrows as readers cannot be identical with the embarrassments of poets, and no critic ever makes a just and dignified assertion of priority. In urging criticism to become more "antithetical," I only urge it farther upon a road already taken. In relation to the poets we are not ephebes wrestling with the dead, but more nearly necromancers, straining to hear the dead sing. These mighty dead are our Sirens, but they are not singing to castrate us. As we listen, we need to remember the Sirens' own sorrows, the anxieties in them that made anxieties for others, though not for ourselves.

I am using the term "antithetical" in its rhetorical meaning: the juxtaposition of contrasting ideas in balanced or parallel structures, phrases, words. Yeats, following Nietzsche, used the term to describe a kind of man, a quester who seeks his own opposite. Freud used it to account for the opposed meanings of primal words:

. . . the strange tendency of the dream-work to disregard negation and to express contraries by identical means of representation . . . this habit of the dream-work . . . exactly tallies with a peculiarity in the oldest languages known to us. . . . In these compound-words contradictory concepts are quite intentionally combined, not in order to express, by means of the combination of the two, the meaning of one of its contradictory members, which alone would have meant the same. . . . In the agreement between that peculiarity of the dream-work . . . and this . . . we may see a confirmation of our supposition in regard to the regressive, archaic character of thought-expression in dreams. . . .

We cannot assume that poetry is a compulsion neurosis. But the lifelong relation of ephebe to precursor can be one. An intense degree of ambivalence characterizes the compulsion neurosis, and from this ambivalence rises a pattern of saving atonement which, in the process of poetic misprision, becomes a quasi-ritual that determines the succession of phases in the poetic life-cycle of strong makers. Angus Fletcher, the demonic allegorist, splendidly remarks that the language of taboo for poets *is* the vocabulary of Freud's "antithetical primal words." In his study of Spenser, Fletcher characterizes the Romantic quester as demanding "a mental space, a referential vacuum, to fill with his own visions." The quester, who finds all space filled with his precursor's visions, resorts to the language of taboo, so as to clear a mental space for himself. It is this language of taboo, this antithetical use of the precursor's primal words, that must serve as the basis for an antithetical criticism.

As students pursuing Poetic Influence we advance now to the *tessera* or link, a different and subtler kind of revisionary ratio. In the *tessera,* the later poet provides what his imagination tells him would complete the otherwise "truncated" precursor poem and poet, a "completion" that is as much misprision as a revisionary swerve is. I take the term *tessera* from the psychoanalyst Jacques Lacan, whose own revisionary relationship to Freud might be given as an instance of *tessera*. In his *Discours de Rome* (1953), Lacan cites a remark of Mallarmé's, which "compares the common use of Language to the exchange of a coin whose obverse and reverse no longer bear any but worn effigies, and which people pass from hand to hand 'in silence.' " Applying this to the discourse, however reduced, of the analytic subject, Lacan says: "This metaphor is sufficient to remind us that the Word, even when almost completely worn out, retains its value as a *tessera*." Lacan's translator, Anthony Wilden, comments that this "allusion is to the function of the *tessera* as a token of recognition, or 'password.' The *tessera* was employed in the early mystery religions where fitting together again the two halves of a broken piece of pottery was used as a means of recognition by the initiates." In this sense of a completing link, the *tessera* represents any later poet's attempt to persuade himself (and us) that the precursor's Word would be worn out if not redeemed as a newly fulfilled and enlarged Word of the ephebe.

Stevens abounds in *tesserae,* for antithetical completion is his central relation to his American Romantic precursors. At the close of *The Sleepers,* in its final version, Whitman identifies night and the mother:

I too pass from the night,
I stay a while away O night, but I return to you again
   and love you.

Why should I be afraid to trust myself to you?
I am not afraid, I have been well brought forward by you,
I love the rich running day, but I do not desert her in
   whom I lay so long,
I know not how I came of you and I know not where I go
   with you, but I know I came well and shall go well.

I will stop only a time with the night, and rise betimes,
I will duly pass the day O my mother, and duly return
    to you.

Stevens antithetically completes Whitman by *The Owl
in the Sarcophagus,* his elegy for his friend Henry Church,
which can best be read as a large *tessera* in relation to
The Sleepers. Where Whitman identifies night and the
mother with good death, Stevens establishes an identity
between good death and a larger maternal vision, opposed
to night because she contains all the memorable evidence
of change, of what we have seen in our long day, though
she has transformed the seen into knowledge:

> She held men closely with discovery,
>
> Almost as speed discovers, in the way
> Invisible change discovers what is changed,
> In the way what was has ceased to be what is.
>
> It was not her look but a knowledge that she had.
> She was a self that knew, an inner thing,
> Subtler than look's declaiming, although she moved
>
> With a sad splendor, beyond artifice,
> Impassioned by the knowledge that she had,
> There on the edges of oblivion.
>
> O exhalation, O fling without a sleeve
> And motion outward, reddened and resolved
> From sight, in the silence that follows her last word—

It seems true that British poets swerve from their pre-
cursors, while American poets labor rather to "complete"
their fathers. The British are more genuinely revisionists
of one another, but we (or at least most of our post-Emer-
sonian poets) tend to see our fathers as not having dared
enough. Yet both revisionary modes reduce in regard to

the precursors. And it is this reductiveness which I judge to offer us our largest clues for practical criticism, for the endless quest of "how to read."

By "reductiveness" I mean a kind of misprision that is a radical misinterpretation in which the precursor is regarded as an over-idealizer, major instances of which would include the writings of Yeats on Blake and Shelley, of Stevens on all the Romantics from Coleridge to Whitman, and of Lawrence on Hardy and Whitman, to mention only the strongest of modern poets in English. Yet it startles me to observe this pattern of reductiveness wherever ephebes comment upon precursors from the High Romantics until now, and not just in the wintry phases of Stevens and other moderns. Shelley was a skeptic, and a kind of visionary materialist; Browning, his ephebe, was a believer and a fierce idealist in metaphysics, yet Browning on Shelley is a reducer, who insists upon "correcting" the excessive metaphysical idealism of his poetic father. As the poets swerve downward in time, they deceive themselves into believing they are tougher-minded than their precursors. This is akin to that critical absurdity which salutes each new generation of bards as being somehow closer to the common language of ordinary men than the last was. The study of poetic influence as anxiety and saving misprision should help to free us from these more absurd myths (or gossip grown old) of literary pseudohistory.

I propose, though, a more positive use for the study of misprision, an antithetical practical criticism as opposed to all the primary criticisms now in vogue. Rousseau remarks that no man can enjoy fully his own selfhood without the aid of others, and an antithetical criticism must found itself upon this realization as being each strong poet's largest motive for metaphor. "Every invention," Malraux says, "is an answer," which I interpret to mean an attempt at the overwhelming confidence of a Leonardo, who was capable of asserting that "He is a poor disciple who does not excell his master." But time has darkened such confidence, and we need to begin again in realizing for how long and how profoundly art has been menaced by greater art, and how late our own poets have come in the story.

All criticisms that call themselves primary vacillate between tautology—in which the poem is and means itself—and reduction—in which the poem means something that is not itself a poem. Antithetical criticism must begin by denying both tautology and reduction, a denial best delivered by the assertion that the meaning of a poem can only be a poem, but *another poem—a poem not itself.* And not a poem chosen with total arbitrariness, but any central poem by an indubitable precursor, even if the ephebe *never read* that poem. Source study is wholly irrelevant here; we are dealing with primal words, but antithetical meanings, and an ephebe's best misinterpretations may well be of poems he has never read.

"Be me but not me" is the paradox of the precursor's implicit charge to the ephebe. Less intensely, his poem says to its descendant poem: "Be like me but unlike me." If there were no ways of subverting this double bind, every ephebe would develop into a poetic version of a schizophrenic. As the pragmaticists of human communication, following Gregory Bateson, say, the double bind "must be disobeyed to be obeyed; if it is a definition of self or the other, the person thereby defined is this kind of person only if he is not, and is not if he is." An individual in the double bind situation is punished for correct perceptions. "The paradoxical injunction . . . *bankrupts choice itself,* nothing is possible, and a self-perpetuating oscillating series is set in motion" (see *Pragmatics of Human Communication* by Watzlawick, Beavin, and Jackson).

Now, it ought to be clear that I am invoking an analogue only, but what I have termed the ephebe's perverseness, his revisionary movements of *clinamen* and *tessera,* are precisely what keeps this double bind situation an analogue rather than an identity. If the ephebe is to avoid over-determination, he needs to forsake correct perception of the poems he values most. Since poetry (like dream-work) is regressive and archaic anyway, and since the precursor is never absorbed as a part of the superego (the Other who commands us) but as part of the id, it is "natural" for the ephebe to *misinterpret.* Even the dream-work is a message or a translation, and so a kind of communication, but a poem is communication deliberately twisted askew, turned about. It is a *mistranslation* of its precursors. Despite all its efforts, it will be always a dyad and not a monad, but a dyad in rebellion against the horror of one-way communication, that is, of the fantasy double bind of wrestling with the mighty dead. Yet the strongest poets deserve a qualifying panegyric at this point in the downward and outward Fall of Poetic Influence.

By "poetic influence" I do not mean the transmission of ideas and images from earlier to later poets. This is indeed just "something that happens," and whether such transmission causes anxiety in the later poets is merely a matter of temperament and circumstances. These are fair materials for source-hunters and biographers, and have little to do with my concern. Ideas and images belong to discursiveness and to history, and are scarcely unique to poetry. Yet a poet's stance, his Word, his imaginative identity, his whole being, *must* be unique to him, and remain unique, or he will perish, as a poet, if ever even he has managed his re-birth into poetic incarnation. But this fundamental stance is as much also his precursor's as any man's fundamental nature is also his father's, however transformed, however turned about. Temperament and circumstance, however fortunate, cannot avail here, in a post-Cartesian consciousness and universe, where there are no intermediate stages between mind and outward nature. The riddle of the Sphinx, for poets, is not just the riddle of the Primal Scene and the mystery of human origins, but the darker riddle of imaginative priority. It is not enough for the poet to answer the riddle; he must persuade himself (and his idealized reader) that the riddle could not have been formulated without him.

Yet, I accept finally (because I must) the massive exception of the *strongest* post-Enlightenment poets, since these few (Milton, Goethe, Hugo) were the most triumphant of modern wrestlers with the dead. But that perhaps is how we can define the greatest, weak as they seem beside Homer, Isaiah, Lucretius, Dante, Shakespeare, who came before the Cartesian engulfment, the flooding-out of a greater mode of consciousness. The burden for the critic of poetic misprision is most powerfully stated by Kierkegaard, in his Panegyric upon Abraham:

> Everyone shall be remembered, but each became great in proportion to his expectation. One became great by expecting the possible; another by expecting the eternal, but he who expected the impossible became greater than all. Everyone shall be remembered, but each was great in proportion to the greatness of that with which he strove.

Kierkegaard might have the last word here, to chastise the faithless critic, yet how many poets still-to-come can deserve this great injunction? Who can bear this heavy splendor, and how will we know him when he comes? Yet, hear Kierkegaard:

> He who will not work does not get the bread but remains deluded, as the gods deluded Orpheus with an airy figure in place of the loved one, deluded him because he was effeminate, not courageous, because he was a cithara-player, not a

man. Here it is of no use to have Abraham for one's father,
nor to have seventeen ancestors— he who will not work
must take note of what is written about the maidens of Is-
rael, for he gives birth to wind, but he who is willing to
work gives birth to his own father.

Yet Kierkegaard's father here is Isaiah, preternaturally
strong poet, and the text cited shatters where Kierkegaard
seeks to comfort. Perhaps the last word lies with the anxi-
ety of influence after all, and with Isaiah's prophecy of the
return of the precursors. What follows did not make Kier-
kegaard anxious, yet it is the dismay of poets:

Like as a woman with child, that draweth near the time
of her delivery, is in pain, and crieth out in her pangs; so
have we been in thy sight, O Lord.

We have been with child, we have been in pain, we have
as it were brought forth wind; we have not wrought any de-
liverance in the earth; neither have the inhabitants of the
world fallen.

Thy dead men shall live, together with my dead body
shall they arise. Awake and sing, ye that dwell in dust: for
thy dew is as the dew of herbs, and the earth shall cast out
the dead.

Three

If the young man had believed in repetition, of what might he not have been capable? What inwardness he might have attained!

KIERKEGAARD

Kenosis

or REPETITION
AND DISCONTINUITY

The *unheimlich,* or "unhomely" as the "uncanny," is perceived wherever we are reminded of our inner tendency to yield to obsessive patterns of action. Overruling the pleasure principle, the *daemonic* in oneself yields to a "repetition compulsion." A man and a woman meet, scarcely talk, enter into a covenant of mutual rendings; rehearse again what they find they have known together before, and yet there was no before. Freud, *unheimlich* here in his insight, maintains that "every emotional affect, whatever its quality, is transformed by repression into morbid anxiety." Among cases of anxiety, Freud finds the class of the *uncanny,* "in which the anxiety can be shown to come from something repressed which *recurs.*" But this "unhomely" might as well be called "the homely," he observes, "for this uncanny is in reality nothing new or foreign, but something familiar and old-established in the mind that has been estranged only by the process of repression."

I offer the special case of the anxiety of influence as a

variety of the uncanny. A man's unconscious fear of castration manifests itself as an apparently physical trouble in his eyes; a poet's fear of ceasing to be a poet frequently manifests itself also as a trouble of his vision. Either he sees *too clearly,* with a tyranny of sharp fixation, as though his eyes asserted themselves against the rest of him as well as against the world, or else his vision becomes veiled, and he sees all things through an estranging mist. One seeing breaks and deforms the seen; the other, at most, beholds a bright cloud.

Critics, in their secret hearts, love continuities, but he who lives with continuity alone cannot be a poet. The God of poets is not Apollo, who lives in the rhythm of recurrence, but the bald gnome Error, who lives at the back of a cave; and skulks forth only at irregular intervals, to feast upon the mighty dead, in the dark of the moon. Error's little cousins, Swerve and Completion, never come into his cave, but they harbor dim memories of having been born there, and they live in the half-apprehension that they will rest at last by coming home to the cave to die. Meanwhile, they too love continuity, for only there have they scope. Except for the desperate poets, only the Ideal or Truly Common reader loves discontinuity, and such a reader still waits to be born.

Poetic misprision, historically a health, is individually a sin against continuity, against the only authority that matters, property or the priority of having named something first. Poetry is property, as politics is property. Hermes ages into a bald gnome, calls himself Error, and founds *commerce.* Intrapoetic relations are neither commerce nor theft, unless you can conceive of family romance as a politics of commerce, or as the dialectic of theft it becomes in Blake's *The Mental Traveller.* But the joyless wisdom of the family romance has little patience for such minor entities as might entertain economists of the spirit. Those

would be generous, little errors, and not grand Error it-
self. The largest Error we can hope to meet and make is
every ephebe's fantasia: quest antithetically enough, and
live to beget yourself.

Night brings each solitary brooder the apparent recom-
pense of a proper background, even as Death, which they
so wrongly dread, properly befriends all strong poets.
Leaves become muted cries, and actual cries are not
heard. Continuities start with the dawn, and no poet *qua*
poet could afford to heed Nietzsche's great injunction:
"Try to live as though it were morning." As poet, the
ephebe must try to live as though it were midnight, a sus-
pended midnight. For the ephebe's first sensation, as
newly incarnated poet, is that of *having been thrown,* out-
ward and downward, by the same glory whose apprehen-
sion *found him,* and made him a poet. The ephebe's first
realm is ocean, or by the side of ocean, and he knows he
reached the element of water through a fall. What is in-
stinctual in him would hold him there, but the antitheti-
cal impulse will bring him out and send him inland,
questing for the fire of his own stance.

Most of what we call poetry—since the Enlightenment
anyway—is this questing for fire, that is, for discontinuity.
Repetition belongs to the watery shore, and Error comes
only to those who go beyond discontinuity, on the airy
journey up into a fearful freedom of weightlessness. Pro-
metheanism, or the quest for *poetic strength,* moves be-
tween the antinomies of *thrown-ness* (which is repetition)
and extravagance (Binswangerian *Verstiegenheit* or *poetic
madness,* or true Error). This is merely cyclic quest, and
its only goal and glory—necessarily—is to fail. The
handful—since the old, great ones—who break this cycle
and live, enter into a counter-sublime, a poetry of earth,
but such a handful (Milton, Goethe, Hugo) are sub-gods.
The strong poets of our time, in English, who enter

greatly into the contest of wrestling with the dead, never go so far as to enter this fourth stage or poetry of earth. Ephebes abound, a double handful manage the Promethean quest, and three or four attain the poetry of discontinuity (Hardy, Yeats, Stevens) in which a poem of the air is achieved.

Where it, the precursor's poem, is there let my poem be; this is the rational formula of every strong poet, for the poetic father has been absorbed into the id, rather than into the superego. The capable poet stands to his precursor rather as Eckhart (or Emerson) stood to God; not as part of the Creation, but as the best part, the uncreated substance, of the Soul. Conceptually the central problem for the latecomer necessarily is *repetition,* for repetition dialectically raised to re-creation is the ephebe's road of excess, leading away from the horror of finding himself to be only a copy or a replica.

Repetition as the recurrence of images from our own past, obsessive images against which our present affections vainly struggle, is one of the prime antagonists that psychoanalysis courageously engaged. Repetition, to Freud, was primarily a mode of compulsion, and reduced to the death instinct by way of inertia, regression, entropy. Fenichel, grim encyclopaedist of the Freudian psychodynamics, follows the Founder in allowing for an "active" repetition in order to gain mastery, but also in emphasizing "undoing" repetition, the neurotic trauma so much more vivid to Freud's imagination. Fenichel distinguishes, as best he can, "undoing" from other defense mechanisms:

> In reaction formation, an attitude is taken that contradicts the original one; in undoing, one more step is taken. Something positive is done which, actually or magically, is the opposite of something which, again actually or in imagination, was done before. . . . The idea of expiation itself is

nothing but an expression of belief in the possibility of a magical undoing.

The compulsion here remains that of repetition, but with a reversal of *unconscious* meaning. In the isolation of an idea from its original emotional investment, repetition also remains dominant. "Beyond the pleasure principle," in Freud's famous phrase, is a dark area in any psychic context, but peculiarly dark in the realms of poetry, which must give pleasure. The hero of *Beyond the Pleasure Principle*, a boy of eighteen months playing his game of *fort!—da!*, masters his mother's disappearances by dramatizing the cycle of her loss and her return. To make of the play-impulse another instance of repetition compulsion was another audacity on Freud's part, but not so audacious as the great leap of ascribing all repetition impulse to a regressive instinct whose pragmatic aim was dying.

Lacan, himself a prodigious leaper, tells us that "in the same way as the compulsion to repeat . . . has in view nothing less than the historizing temporality of the experience of transference, so does the death instinct essentially express the limit of the historical function of the subject." So Lacan sees the *fort!—da!* as the humanizing acts of the child's verbal imagination, in which subjectivity combines its own abdication and the birth of the symbol, "the acts of occultation which Freud, in a flash of genius, revealed to us so that we might recognize in them that the moment in which desire becomes human is also that in which the child is born into Language."

Lacan's sense of "this limit," our death, represents it as "the past which reveals itself reversed in repetition." Encroaching upon his curious blend of Freud and Heidegger is the great shadow of the Kierkegaardian repetition, "the exhaustion of being which consumes itself," as Lacan

phrases it. Freudian repetition is interpretable only dual-
istically, like all psychoanalytic notions, for Freud expects
us always to separate manifest from latent content. Kierke-
gaard, too dialectical for such merely Romantic irony, for-
mulated a "repetition" closer to the ironies of poetic mis-
prision than the Freudian "undoing" or "isolation"
mechanisms could allow.

Kierkegaardian repetition never *happens*, but *breaks
forth* or *steps forth,* since it "is recollected forwards," like
God's Creation of the universe.

> If God himself had not willed repetition, the world
> would never have come into existence. He would either
> have followed the light plans of hope, or he would have re-
> called it all and conserved it in recollection. This he did not
> do, therefore the world endures, and it endures for the fact
> that it is a repetition.

The life which has been *now becomes.* Kierkegaard says
that the dialectic of repetition is "easy," but this is one of
his genial jokes. His best joke about repetition is also his
first, and seems to me a grand introduction to the dialectic
of misprision:

> Repetition and recollection are the same movement, only
> in opposite directions; for what is recollected has been, is re-
> peated backwards whereas repetition properly so called is
> recollected forwards. Therefore repetition, if it is possible,
> makes a man happy, whereas recollection makes him
> unhappy—provided he gives himself time to live and does
> not at once, in the very moment of birth, try to find a pre-
> text for stealing out of life, alleging, for example, that he
> has forgotten something.

Joking at Plato's expense, the theorist of repetition pro-
poses a possible but not a perfect love, that is, the only
love that will not make one unhappy, love of repetition.

Perfect love is to love even where one has been made unhappy, but repetition belongs to the imperfect that is our paradise. The strong poet survives because he lives the discontinuity of an "undoing" and an "isolating" repetition, but he would cease to be a poet unless he kept living the continuity of "recollecting forwards," of breaking forth into a freshening that yet repeats his precursors' achievements.

Misprision, we can now amend, is indeed a doing amiss (and taking amiss) of what the precursors did, but "amiss" has itself a dialectical meaning here. What the precursors did has thrown the ephebe into the outward and downward motion of repetition, a repetition that the ephebe soon understands must be both undone and dialectically affirmed, and these simultaneously. The mechanism of undoing is easily available, as all psychic defenses are, but the process of repeating by recollecting forwards is not easily learned. When the ephebe calls upon the Muse to help him remember the future, he is asking her for aid in repetition, but hardly in the sense that children ask a storyteller to keep to the same story. The child learning a story, as Schachtel suggests in his *Metamorphosis,* seeks to *rely* upon the story, rather as we rely upon a favorite poem to keep the same words the next time we open that particular book. Object constancy makes exploration by acts of focal attention possible, and Schachtel relies upon this dependence when he optimistically disputes Freud's insistence upon the prevalence of repetition compulsion in the play of children. At the core of Schachtel's argument is a deep disagreement with Freud's profoundly reductive theory of the origin of thought. Thought's precursor, to Freud, is always and only a hallucinatory satisfaction of need, a phantasmagoria in which wish fulfillment is displaced and the ego seeks more autonomy from the id than it is capable of achieving.

For the ego experiences "having been thrown" in relation to the id, and not to the censorious superego. The ego psychologists may have been correct in their revision of Freud, but not from the standpoint of the critic of literature, who rightly must ascribe the energies of creativity to an area (however we name it) which has outered the ego to meet the whole world of the Not-Me, or perhaps better, the Pascalian "infinite immensity of spaces of which I am ignorant, and which know me not." Cast out into the external magnitudes of Cartesian matter, the ego learns its own solitude, and seeks compensatingly for an illusory autonomy, for what will deceive it into some sense of being made free:

> What makes us free is the knowledge who we were, what we have become; where we were, wherein we have been thrown; whereto we speed, wherefrom we are redeemed; what is birth and what rebirth.

This Valentinian formula, Hans Jonas remarks, "makes no provision for a *present* on whose content knowledge may dwell and, in beholding, stay the forward thrust." Jonas compares the Gnostic "wherein we have been thrown" to the Heideggerian *Geworfenheit* and the Pascalian "cast out." A further comparison is suggested by the situation of every post-Cartesian ephebe, who is a Gnostic frequently in spite of himself. Perhaps, after all, Yeats's dreadful greatness stems from his voluntary Gnosticism, and his deep comprehension of how badly he needed it as poet.

When we cease to expect, we may be rewarded. Keats is so moving because he is so detached towards what is required of him as poet, yet so faithful in the fulfillment of requirements. But any poem—even a perfect one, like Keats's *To Autumn*—is a massing of misplacements.

Keats, even Keats, must be a prophet of discontinuity, for whom experience at last is only another form of paralysis. Between the poet and his vision of the true, unknown god (or himself healed, rendered original, and pure) intervene the precursors as so many Gnostic archons. Our young, a while ago, were pseudo-Gnostics, believing in an essential purity that constituted their true selves and that could not be touched by mere natural experience. Strong poets must believe something like that, and should always be condemned by a humanist morality, for strong poets necessarily are perverse, "necessarily" here meaning as if obsessed, as if manifesting repetition compulsion. "Perverse" literally means "to be turned the wrong way"; but to be turned the right way in regard to the precursor means not to swerve at all, so any bias or inclination perforce must be perverse in *relation to the precursor,* unless context itself (such as one's own surrounding literary orthodoxy) allows one to be *an avatar of the perverse,* as the French line Baudelaire-Mallarmé-Valéry was of Poe, or Frost of Emerson. To swerve (Anglo-Saxon *sweorfan*) has a root meaning of "to wipe off, file down, or polish," and, in usage, "to deviate, to leave the straight line, to turn aside (from law, duty, custom)."

Yet the strong poet's imagination *cannot see itself as perverse;* its own inclination must be health, the true priority. Hence the *clinamen,* whose fundamental assumption is that the precursor went wrong by *failing to swerve,* at just such a bias, just then and there, at one angle of vision, whether acute or obtuse. Yet this is distressing, and not just to the sweet-at-heart in oneself. If the imagination's gift comes necessarily from the perversity of the spirit, then the living labyrinth of literature is built upon the ruin of every impulse most generous in us. So apparently it is and must be—we are wrong to have founded a humanism directly upon literature itself, and the phrase "humane letters" is an oxymoron. A humanism might still be founded upon a completer *study of literature* than we have yet achieved, but never upon literature itself, or any idealized mirroring of its implicit categories. The strong imagination comes to its painful birth through savagery and misrepresentation. The only humane virtue we can hope to teach through a more advanced study of literature than we have now is the social virtue of detachment from one's own imagination, recognizing always that such detachment made absolute destroys any individual imagination.

Where there is detachment in confronting one's own imagination, discontinuity is impossible. Where desire ends, repetition pulses on, whether or not re-imagined. There are no names, Valéry said, for those things among which a man is most truly alone; and Stevens urges his ephebe to throw away the lights, the definitions, in order to find identifications replacing the rotted names that will not grant a context of solitude. This darkness is a discontinuity, in which the ephebe can see again and know the illusion of a fresh priority.

The best passional analogue to this discontinuity is not first love, but first jealousy, "first" meaning consciously first. Jealousy, Camus has Caligula taunt a cuckolded husband, is a disease compounded of vanity and imagination. Jealousy, any strong poet would tell Caligula, is founded on our fear that there will not be enough time, indeed that there is more love than can be put into time. Discontinuity, for poets, is found not so much in spots of time as in moments of space, where repetition is voided, as though the economics of pleasure had no relation to the release of tension but only to our being lost in mind.

Let us return to Freud's still-startling late manifesto of 1920, *Beyond the Pleasure Principle,* which relates erotic foreplay to recurrent neuroses, and both to little Ernst

Freud's game of maternal abandonment, the celebrated *fort!—da!*, so dear to the re-imaginings of Lacan. All these are "repetition compulsions," and in the final Freudian vision, all are *daemonic,* self-destructive, and in the worship of the god Thanatos:

> Perhaps we have adopted the belief [the death instinct] because there is some comfort in it. If we are to die ourselves, and first to lose in death those who are dear to us, it is easier to submit to a remorseless law of nature, to the sublime necessity, than to a chance which might perhaps have been escaped. . . .

That is late Freud, but might be the late Emerson of *The Conduct of Life,* with his grim worship of the Beautiful Necessity. Both Freud and Emerson associate this sublime necessity with aggression, and oppose to it an Eros, though Freud's Eros is an enlarged vision of the libido, and Emerson's a late, largely undefined version of the Oversoul. Neither of them, at the end, was less than ambivalent towards the ego's mechanisms of defense against the repetitions driving us to Thanatos. But, in the Freudian accounts of such mechanisms, and particularly in what I have already cited from Fenichel, a theoretical basis is provided for criticism to describe the strong poets' defense against repetition, their saving (but also dooming) adventure in discontinuity.

To the study of revisionary ratios that characterize intra-poetic relationships, I now add a third: *kenosis* or "emptying," at once an "undoing" and an "isolating" movement of the imagination. I take *kenosis* from St. Paul's account of Christ "humbling" himself from God to man. In strong poets, the *kenosis* is a revisionary act in which an "emptying" or "ebbing" takes place *in relation to the precursor.* This "emptying" is a liberating discontinuity, and makes possible a kind of poem that a simple repetition of the precursor's afflatus or godhood could not allow. "Undoing" the precursor's strength *in oneself* serves also to "isolate" the self from the precursor's stance, and saves the latecomer-poet from becoming taboo in and to himself. Freud emphasizes the relation of defense mechanisms to the entire area of the taboo, and we note the relevance to the *kenosis* of the context of touching and washing taboos.

Why is influence, which might be a health, more generally an anxiety where strong poets are concerned? Do strong poets gain or lose more, *as poets,* in their wrestling with their ghostly fathers? Do *clinamen, tessera, kenosis,* and all other revisionary ratios that misinterpret or metamorphose precursors help poets to individuate themselves, truly to be themselves, or do they distort the poetic sons quite as much as they do the fathers? I am predicating that these revisionary ratios have the same function in intra-poetic relations that defense mechanisms have in our psychic life. Do the mechanisms of defense, in our daily lives, damage us more than the repetition compulsions from which they seek to defend us?

Freud, highly dialectical here, is clearest I think in the powerful late essay, "Analysis Terminable and Interminable" (1937). If for his "ego" we substitute the ephebe, and for his "id" the precursor, then he gives us a formula for the ephebe's dilemma:

> For quite a long time flight and an avoidance of a dangerous situation serve as expedients in the face of external danger, until the individual is finally strong enough to remove the menace by actively modifying reality. But one cannot flee from oneself and no flight avails against danger from within; hence the ego's defensive mechanisms are condemned to falsify the inner perception, *so that it transmits to us only an imperfect and travestied picture of our id. In*

its relations with the id the ego is paralyzed by its restrictions or blinded by its errors, and the result in the sphere of psychical events may be compared to the progress of a poor walker in a country which he does not know.

The purpose of the defensive mechanisms is to avert dangers. It cannot be disputed that they are successful; it is doubtful whether the ego can altogether do without them during its development, but it is also certain that they themselves may become dangerous. Not infrequently it turns out that the ego has paid too high a price for the services which these mechanisms render. [my italics; not Freud's]

This melancholy vision ends with the adult ego, at its strongest, defending itself against vanished dangers and even seeking substitutes for the vanished originals. In the *agon* of the strong poet, the achieved substitutes tend to be earlier versions of the ephebe himself, who in some sense laments a glory he never had. Without as yet abandoning the Freudian model, let us examine more closely the crucial mechanisms of "undoing" and "isolating," before returning to the darkness I have called *kenosis* or "emptying."

Fenichel relates "undoing" to expiation, a washing-clean that still obeys the taboo of washing, and which therefore intends to do the opposite of the compulsive act yet paradoxically performs the same act with an opposite unconscious meaning. Artistic sublimation, on this view, is connected to attitudes that intend an undoing of imaginative destructions. "Isolating" keeps apart what belongs together, preserving traumata but abandoning their emotional meanings, while obeying the taboo against touching. Spatial and temporal distortions frequently abound in such phenomena of isolation, as we might expect from the connection here to the primordial taboo on touching.

Kenosis is a more ambivalent movement than *clinamen* or *tessera,* and necessarily brings poems more deeply into the realms of antithetical meanings. For, in *kenosis*, the artist's battle against art has been lost, and the poet falls or ebbs into a space and time that confine him, even as he undoes the precursor's pattern by a deliberate, willed loss in continuity. His stance *appears* to be that of his precursor (as Keats's stance appears to be Milton's in the first *Hyperion*), but the meaning of the stance is undone; the stance is *emptied* of its priority, which is a kind of godhood, and the poet holding it becomes more isolated, not only from his fellows, but from the continuity of his own self.

What is the use of this notion of poetic *kenosis,* to the reader attempting to describe any poem he feels compelled to describe? The ratios *clinamen* and *tessera* may be useful in aligning (and disaligning) elements in disparate poems, but this third ratio seems more applicable to poets than to poems. Since, as readers, we need to tell the dancer from the dance, the singer from his song, how are we aided in our difficult enterprise by this idea of a self-emptying that seeks to defend against the father, yet radically undoes the son? Is the *kenosis* of Shelley in his *Ode to the West Wind* an undoing, an isolating of Wordsworth or of Shelley? Who is emptied more fearfully in Whitman's *As I Ebb'd with the Ocean of Life,* Emerson or Whitman? When Stevens confronts the terrible auroras, is it his autumn or Keats's that is emptied of its humanizing solace? Ammons, walking the dunes of Corsons Inlet, empties himself of an Overall, now acknowledged to be beyond him, but does not the poem's meaning turn upon its conviction that Emerson's Overall was beyond even that sage? The palinode seems to be inevitable in the later phases of any Romantic poet's progress, but is it his own song he must sing over again in reversal? Dante, Chaucer, even Spenser can make their own recantation into poetry, but Milton, Goethe, Hugo recant their precursors' errors rather more than their own. With more ambivalent modern poets, even poets as strong as Blake, Wordsworth, Baudelaire, Rilke, Yeats, Stevens, every *kenosis* voids a precursor's powers, as though a magical undoing-isolating sought to save the Egotistical Sublime at a father's expense. *Kenosis,* in this poetic and revisionary sense, appears to be an act of self-abnegation, yet tends to make the fathers pay for their own sins, and perhaps for those of the sons also.

I arrive therefore at the pragmatic formula: "Where the precursor was, there the ephebe shall be, but by the discontinuous mode of emptying the precursor of *his* divinity, while appearing to empty himself of his own." However plangent or even despairing the poem of *kenosis,* the ephebe takes care to fall soft, while the precursor falls hard.

We need to stop thinking of any poet as an autonomous ego, however solipsistic the strongest of poets may be. Every poet is a being caught up in a dialectical relationship (transference, repetition, error, communication) with another poet or poets. In the archetypal *kenosis,* St. Paul found a pattern that no poet whatever could bear to emulate, as poet:

> Let nothing be done through strife or vainglory; but in lowliness of mind let each esteem others better than themselves.
>
> Look not every man on his own things, but every man also on the things of others.
>
> Let this mind be in you, which was also in Christ Jesus:
>
> Who, being in the form of God, thought it not robbery to be equal with God:
>
> But made himself of no reputation, and took upon him the form of a servant, and was made in the likeness of men:
>
> And being found in fashion as a man, he humbled himself, and became obedient unto death. . . .

Against this *kenosis*, we can set a characteristic *dae-monic* parody of it which is the poetic *kenosis* proper, not so much a humbling of self as of all precursors, and necessarily a defiance unto death. Blake cries out to Tirzah:

> Whate'er is Born of Mortal Birth,
> Must be consumed with the Earth
> To rise from Generation free;
> Then what have I to do with thee?

INTERCHAPTER

A Manifesto for Antithetical Criticism

If to imagine is to misinterpret, which makes all poems antithetical to their precursors, then to imagine after a poet is to learn his own metaphors for his acts of reading. Criticism then necessarily becomes antithetical also, a series of swerves after unique acts of creative misunderstanding.

The first swerve is to learn to read a great precursor poet as his greater descendants compelled themselves to read him.

The second is to read the descendants as if we were their disciples, and so compel ourselves to learn where we must revise them if we are to be found by our own work, and claimed by the living of our own lives.

Neither of these quests is yet Antithetical Criticism.

That begins when we measure the first *clinamen* against the second. Finding just what the accent of deviation is, we proceed to apply it as corrective to the reading of the

first but not the second poet or group of poets. To prac-
tice Antithetical Criticism on the more recent poet or
poets becomes possible only when they have found disci-
ples not ourselves. But these can be critics, and not poets.

It can be objected against this theory that we never
read a poet as poet, but only read one poet in another
poet, or even into another poet. Our answer is manifold:
we deny that there is, was or ever can be a poet as poet—
to a reader. Just as we can never embrace (sexually or oth-
erwise) a single person, but embrace the whole of her or
his family romance, so we can never read a poet without
reading the whole of his or her family romance as poet.
The issue is reduction and how best to avoid it. Rhetori-
cal, Aristotelian, phenomenological, and structuralist criti-
cisms all reduce, whether to images, ideas, given things, or
phonemes. Moral and other blatant philosophical or psy-
chological criticisms all reduce to rival conceptualizations.
We reduce—if at all—to another poem. The meaning of
a poem can only be another poem. This is not a tautology,
not even a deep tautology, since the two poems are not
the same poem, any more than two lives can be the same
life. The issue is true history or rather the true use of it,
rather than the abuse of it, both in Nietzsche's sense.
True poetic history is the story of how poets as poets have
suffered other poets, just as any true biography is the story
of how anyone suffered his own family—or his own dis-
placement of family into lovers and friends.

Summary—Every poem is a misinterpretation of a par-
ent poem. A poem is not an overcoming of anxiety, but is
that anxiety. Poets' misinterpretations or poems are more
drastic than critics' misinterpretations or criticism, but

this is only a difference in degree and not at all in kind. There are no interpretations but only misinterpretations, and so all criticism is prose poetry.

Critics are more or less valuable than other critics only (precisely) as poets are more or less valuable than other poets. For just as a poet must be found by the opening in a precursor poet, so must the critic. The difference is that a critic has more parents. His precursors are poets and critics. But—in truth—so are a poet's precursors, often and more often as history lengthens.

Poetry is the anxiety of influence, is misprision, is a disciplined perverseness. Poetry is misunderstanding, misinterpretation, misalliance.

Poetry (Romance) is Family Romance. Poetry is the enchantment of incest, disciplined by resistance to that enchantment.

Influence is *Influenza*—an astral disease.

If influence were health, who could write a poem? Health is stasis.

Schizophrenia is bad poetry, for the schizophrenic has lost the strength of perverse, wilful, misprision.

Poetry is thus both contraction and expansion; for all the ratios of revision are contracting movements, yet making is an expansive one. Good poetry is a dialectic of revisionary movement (contraction) and freshening outward-going-ness.

The best critics of our time remain Empson and Wilson Knight, for they have misinterpreted more antithetically than all others.

When we say that the meaning of a poem can only be another poem, we may mean a range of poems:

The precursor poem or poems.
The poem we write as our reading.
A rival poem, son or grandson of the same
precursor.
A poem that never got written—that is—
the poem that should have been written by
the poet in question.
A composite poem, made up of these in some
combination.

A poem is a poet's melancholy at his lack of priority. The failure to have begotten oneself is not the cause of the poem, for poems arise out of the illusion of freedom, out of a sense of priority being possible. But the poem—unlike the mind in creation—is a made thing, and as such is an achieved anxiety.

How do we understand an anxiety? By ourselves being anxious. Every deep reader is an Idiot Questioner. He asks, "Who wrote my poem?" Hence Emerson's insistence that: "In every work of genius we recognize our own rejected thoughts—they come back to us with a certain alienated majesty."

Criticism is the discourse of the deep tautology—of the solipsist who knows that what he means is right, and yet that what he says is wrong. Criticism is the art of knowing the hidden roads that go from poem to poem.

Four

And now at last the highest truth on this subject remains unsaid; probably cannot be said; for all that we say is the far-off remembering of the intuition. That thought by what I can now nearest approach to say it, is this. When good is near you, when you have life in yourself, it is not by any known or accustomed way; you shall not discern the footprints of any other; you shall not see the face of man; you shall not hear any name;—the way, the thought, the good, shall be wholly strange and new. It shall exclude example and experience. You take the way from man, not to man. All persons that ever existed are its forgotten ministers. Fear and hope are alike beneath it. There is somewhat low even in hope. In the hour of vision there is nothing that can be called gratitude, nor properly joy. The soul raised over passion beholds identity and eternal causation, perceives the self-existence of Truth and Right, and calms itself with knowing that all things go well. Vast spaces of nature, the Atlantic Ocean, the South Sea; long intervals of time, years, centuries, are of no account. This which I think and feel underlay every former state of life and circumstances, as it does underlie my present, and what is called life and what is called death.

EMERSON, *Self-Reliance*

Daemonization

or THE COUNTER-SUBLIME

The strong new poet must reconcile in himself two truths: "*Ethos* is the *daimon*" and "all things were made through him, and without him was not anything made that was made." Poetry, despite its publicists, is not a struggle against repression but is itself a kind of repression. Poems rise not so much in response to a present time, as even Rilke thought, but in response to other poems. "The times are resistance," said Rilke, to the poet's vision of new worlds and times; but he might better have said: "The precursor poems are resistance," for the *Befreiungen* or new poems rise from a more central tension than Rilke acknowledged. History, to Rilke, was the index of men born too soon, but as a strong poet Rilke would not let himself know that art is the index of men born too late. Not the dialectic between art and society, but the dialectic between art and art, or what Rank was to call the artist's struggle against art; this dialectic governed even Rilke, who outlasted most of his blocking agents, for in him the revisionary ratio of *daemonization* was stronger than in any other poet of our century.

"The Daemons lurk and are dumb," Emerson mused, and they lurk everywhere in him, quite audibly. When the ancients spoke of daemons, they meant also (as Drayton said) "them who for the greatness of mind come near to Gods. For to be born of a celestial Incubus, is nothing else, but to have a great and mighty spirit, far above the earthly weakness of men." The power that makes a man a poet is daemonic, because it is the power that distributes and divides (which is the root meaning of *daeomai*). It distributes our fates, and divides our gifts, compensating wherever it takes from us. This division brings order, confers knowledge, disorders where it knows, blesses with ignorance to create another order. The daemons make by breaking ("Marbles of the dancing floor / Break bitter furies of complexity"), yet all they have are their voices, and that is all that poets have.

Ficino's daemons existed to bring down voices from the planets to favored men. These daemons *were* influence, moving from Saturn to genius below, conveying the most generous of Melancholies. But, truly, the strong poet is never "possessed" by a daemon. When he grows strong, he becomes, and is, a daemon, unless and until he weakens again. "Possession leads to total identification," Angus Fletcher observes. Turning against the precursor's Sublime, the newly strong poet undergoes *daemonization,* a Counter-Sublime whose function suggests *the precursor's relative weakness*. When the ephebe is daemonized, his precursor necessarily is humanized, and a new Atlantic floods outward from the new poet's transformed being.

For the strong poet's Sublime cannot be the reader's Sublime unless each reader's life indeed is a Sublime Allegory also. The Counter-Sublime does not show forth as limitation to the imagination proving its capability. In *this* transport, the only visible object eclipsed or dissolved is the vast image of the precursor, and the mind is wholly happy to be thrown back upon itself. Burke's is the reader's Sublime: a pleasing Terror, with what Martin Price terms "the counterstress of self-preservation." Burke's reader yields to sympathy what he refuses to description; he need *see* only the most indefinite of outlines. In *daemonization,* the augmented poetic consciousness sees clear outline, and yields back to description what it had over-yielded to sympathy. But this "description" is a revisionary ratio, a daemonic vision in which the Great Original remains great but loses his originality, yielding it to the world of the numinous, the sphere of daemonic agency to which his splendor is now reduced. *Daemonization* or the Counter-Sublime is a war between Pride and Pride, and momentarily the power of newness wins.

As a theorist of misprision, I would stop here if I could, to develop the Counter-Sublime as a state-in-itself, without recourse to negative theology. But there is no *daemonization* without an intrusion of the numinous, and no account of this revisionary ratio can exclude the idea of the Holy. Every strong poet might want to say, with Blake and Whitman, that everything that lives is holy, but Blake and Whitman were so fully *daemonized* as not to be representative. In most, there is a context against which the numinous shines forth. This context is a void, emptied or estranged by the poets themselves, while the shining-forth returns us to all the sorrows of divination.

The ephebe learns divination first when he apprehends the appalling energy of his *own* precursor as being at once the Wholly Other yet also a possessing force. This apprehension, which in its early stages seems more the gift of surmise than of divination, is independent of the will and yet is altogether conscious. To divine the glory one already is becomes a mixed blessing when there is deep anxiety whether one has become truly oneself. Yet this sense of glory, should it prove to be an error about life, is neces-

sary for a poet as poet, who must achieve imagination here
by denying the full humanity of imagination. Nietzsche's
powerful wit is appropriate:

> If, in all that he does, he considers the final aimlessness of
> man, his own activity assumes in his eyes the character of
> wastefulness. But to feel one's self just as much wasted as hu-
> manity (and not only as an individual) as we see the single
> blossom of nature wasted, is a feeling above all other feel-
> ings. But who is capable of it? Assuredly only a poet, and
> poets always know how to console themselves.

Negation of the precursor is never possible, since no
ephebe can afford to yield even momentarily to the death
instinct. For poetic divination intends literal immortality,
and any poem may be defined as a side-stepping of a possi-
ble death. The way of man which takes him through nega-
tion is a primal act, the act of repression, in which man
continues to desire, remains purposeful, yet denies desire
or purpose any conscious entertainment in his mind. "Ne-
gation only assists in undoing one of the consequences of
repression—the fact that the subject-matter of the image
in question is unable to enter consciousness. The result is
a kind of intellectual acceptance of what is repressed,
though in all essentials the repression persists." This
Freudian formulation is the exact reverse of *daemoniza-
tion,* and marks another limit that no strong poet can per-
mit himself to accept.

What precisely is "the daemonic" that makes the
ephebe into a strong poet? Any consciousness that will not
negate cannot live with the reality principle. But the ne-
cessity for dying will not allow itself to be evaded forever,
and men do not remain men without repression, however
strongly the repressed returns. The law of Compensation,
Emerson's "nothing is got for nothing," is felt even by

poets, despite their brief moments-of-moments in which truly they are liberating gods. Whatever the Spirit is, there can be no polymorphous perversity of the Spirit, and an evaded repression yields only another repression. "The daemonic," in poets, cannot be distinguished from the anxiety of influence, and this is, alas, a true identity and no similitude. The reader's terror of and in the Sublime is matched by every post-Enlightenment strong poet's anxiety of and in the Counter-Sublime.

Emerson, the unsurpassable prophet of the American Sublime (which is always a Counter-Sublime), would protest most beautifully against our sad murmur that after all there is still the universe of death, our world: ". . . All that you call the world is the shadow of that substance which you are, the perpetual creation of the powers of thought, of those that are dependent and those that are independent of your will. . . . You think me the child of my circumstance: I make my circumstance." With loving respect the student of misprision must murmur back: "You do, you do, but if that circumstance is the poet's stance, ringed about by the living circumference of the precursors, then the shadow of your substance meets and mingles with a greater Shadow." Shelley, with his characteristic English balance, can be cited against Emerson here:

> . . . one great poet is a masterpiece of nature which another not only ought to study but must study. He might as wisely and as easily determine that his mind should no longer be the mirror of all that is lovely in the visible universe, as exclude from his contemplation the beautiful which exists in the writings of a great contemporary. The pretence of doing it would be a presumption in any but the greatest; the effect, even in him, would be strained, unnatural and ineffectual. A poet is the combined product of such internal powers as modify the nature of others; and of such external influences as excite and sustain these powers; he is

not one, but both. Every man's mind is, in this respect, modified by all the objects of nature and art; by every word and every suggestion which he ever admitted to act upon his consciousness; it is the mirror upon which all forms are reflected, and in which they compose one form. Poets, not otherwise than philosophers, painters, sculptors, and musicians, are, in one sense, the creators, and, in another, the creations of their age. From this subjection the loftiest do not escape.

Shelley's subjection, as he knew, was to the precursor who had created (as much as anyone had, even Rousseau) the Spirit of the Age. Against Wordsworth, Shelley became a strong poet, from *Alastor* on, by a new kind of questing flight, an upward movement in which nevertheless the Spirit was thrown outwards and down. Shelley's daemonization was this upward falling away, and more than any poet (even Rilke) Shelley compels us to see him in the company of angels, the daemonic partners of his quest for totality.

Paul de Man, expounding Binswanger, speaks of "the imaginative possibility of what could be called an upward fall," and the subsequent descent, "the possibility of falling and of despondency that follows such moments of flight," or what roughly I have called *kenosis*. Binswangerian *Verstiegenheit* (or "Extravagance," as Jacob Needleman wittily translates it, relying on the root meaning of "wandering beyond limits") is spoken of by de Man as a distinct imaginative danger; but falling upwards we can distinguish as the process, and Extravagance as the state ensuing. Thrown forth by the intoxicating glory of participating in the precursor's strength, the ephebe appears (to himself) to levitate, an experience of afflatus that abandons him upon the heights, risen to an Extravagance that is a "failure of the relationship between height and breadth in the anthropological sense." This is human existence gone too far, the poet's particular melancholy, oddly represented for Binswanger by Ibsen's Solness, who scarcely seems adequate to so large a notion of disproportion. Binswanger's summary is useful if we read it backwards; rescue from Extravagance, he says, is possible only by "outside help," as with the mountain climber too far out upon his precipice to go back. Let us agree that a strong poet, as poet, by definition is beyond "outside help," and purely as poet would be destroyed by it. What Binswanger sees as pathology is merely the perverse health or attained sublimity of the achieved poet.

Van Den Berg, in a startling essay on the significance of human movement, locates three domains that yield such significance: the *landscape,* the *inner self,* the *glance of another.* If we look for the significance of poetic movement, in the sense of a poem's carriage and gestures even as we speak of a human's, this transposes into: *estrangement, solipsism,* the *imagined glance of the precursor.* To appropriate the precursor's landscape for himself, the ephebe must estrange it further from himself. To attain a self yet more inward than the precursor's, the ephebe becomes necessarily more solipsistic. To evade the precursor's imagined glance, the ephebe seeks to confine it in scope, which perversely enlarges the glance, so that it rarely can be evaded. As the small child believes his parents can see him around corners, so the ephebe feels a magical glance attending his every movement. The desired glance is friendly or loving, but the feared glance disapproves, or renders the ephebe unworthy of the highest love, alienates him from the realms of poetry. Moving through landscapes that are mute, or of things that speak to him less often or urgently than they did to the precursor, the ephebe knows also the cost of an increasing inwardness, a greater separation from everything extensive. The loss is of reciprocity with the world, as compared to the precursor's sense of being a man to whom all things spoke.

The thrust of *daemonization* is towards a Counter-Sublime, or what post-Freudian vitalists like Marcuse and Brown evidently hope to mean when they speak of what Freud called a return of the repressed. Shelley, like all strong poets, learned better (as poet, perhaps not as man), and better than any other poet shows us now that the repressed cannot return, not at least in poems. For every Counter-Sublime is purchased by a fresh and greater repression than the precursor's Sublime. *Daemonization* attempts to expand the precursor's power to a principle larger than his own, but pragmatically makes the son more of a daemon and the precursor more of a man. The gloomiest truth of post-Enlightenment poetic history is almost too sour for our humane taste, and all of Nietzsche's dialectical exuberance did not succeed in obscuring a truth we evade for the social good of the academies. The daemon in each of us is the Latecomer; the blinded Oedipus is the human, the total coherence that knows life cannot be justified as an aesthetic phenomenon, even when that life is wholly sacrificed to the aesthetic realm. Schopenhauer, and not Nietzsche, takes the honor here of having confronted the truth, as Nietzsche must have known, even in *The Birth of Tragedy* where he tries to overcome his darker precursor by a direct refutation. Who can fail to perceive in Schopenhauer's description of lyric poetry, Nietzsche says, that it is presented as an art never completely realized? Authentic song—to Schopenhauer— shows a state of mind mixed and divided between mere willing and pure contemplation. As a daemonic son, Nietzsche eloquently protests that the striving individual who seeks his egoistic purposes is only an enemy of art,

and not its source. For Nietzsche, a man is an artist only
to the extent that he is free of individual will "and has be-
come a medium through which the True Subject cele-
brates the True Subject's own redemption in illusion."
Freud, in his beautiful humaneness, followed the earlier
Nietzsche in this highly qualified idealism, but time has
shown Schopenhauer's greater wisdom. For what is the
True Subject but repression? The ego is not the enemy of
art, but rather art's sad brother. Art's True Subject is art's
great antagonist, the terrible Cherub concealed in the id,
for the id is the huge illusion that cannot be redeemed.
The original sin of art, as Nietzsche so wonderfully exem-
plifies, is that a False Tongue vegetates beneath nature,
or to use less Blakean language, that no artist can forgive
his own origins *as artist.*

Freud's vision of repression emphasizes that forgetting
is anything but a liberating process. Every forgotten pre-
cursor becomes a giant of the imagination. Total repres-
sion would be health, but only a god is capable of it.
Every poet desires to be Emerson's liberating god, and in-
creasingly every poet fails. In Christian vision, our guilt
rises from repression of our higher nature or moral heri-
tage. In Freudian vision, our guilt stems from instinctual
repression, the balking of lower nature. In poetic vision,
guilt comes from repression of our middle nature, the
ground where morals and instincts must meet and sub-
sume one another. *Daemonization,* which commences as a
revisionary ratio of de-individuating the precursor, ends
by the dubious triumph of yielding to him the whole of
the ephebe's middle ground, or common humanity. In re-
lation to the precursor, the latecomer poet compels him-
self to a fresh repression at once moral and instinctual.
One of the lunatic paradoxes of post-Miltonic poetry in
English is that Milton appears (and perhaps was) freer of

guilt, both moral and instinctual, when contrasted to Blake, Wordsworth, Shelley, or even to Keats among the greatest of his descendants.

When Shelley re-wrote the "Intimations" ode as his *Hymn to Intellectual Beauty,* he underwent a *daemonization* that burdened him, morally and instinctually, with a program too intense even for his curiously tough and swift spirit to carry through. Strong poems that too explicitly re-write precursor poems tend to become *poems of conversion,* and conversion is not an aesthetic phenomenon, even when the convert is moving from Apollo to Dionysus, or back again. Here it is helpful to remember one of Nietzsche's remarkable destructions of his own central insights:

> While the transport of the Dionysiac state, with its suspension of all the ordinary barriers of existence, lasts, it carries with it a Lethean element in which everything that has been experienced by the individual is drowned. This chasm of oblivion separates the quotidian reality from the Dionysiac. But as soon as that quotidian reality enters consciousness once more it is viewed with loathing, and the consequence is an ascetic, abulic state of mind.

On this view, all influx is loss, and the price of transport is a revulsion that the aesthetic realm cannot contain. From naming a god, Whitman passes to a disgust that prevents any naming whatsoever:

O baffled, balk'd, bent to the very earth,
Oppress'd with myself that I have dared to open my mouth,
Aware now that amid all that blab whose echoes recoil upon
    me I have not once had the least idea who or what I am.
But that before all my arrogant poems the real Me stands yet
    untouch'd, untold, altogether unreach'd. . . .

If we start again with the Freudian idea that tradition is "equivalent to repressed material in the mental life of the individual," then the function of *daemonization* is rightly to augment repression, by absorbing the precursor more thoroughly into tradition than his own courageous individuation should allow him to be absorbed. Nietzsche celebrates Oedipus as another exemplar of Dionysiac wisdom because he breaks "the spell of present and future, the rigid law of individuation," but here the Nietzschean irony is presumably most dialectical. The ephebe wrestling with and *daemonizing* the past is not Oedipus the diviner, *who could see,* but blinded Oedipus, darkened by revelation. *Daemonization,* like all mythification of the fathers, is an individuating movement purchased by withdrawal from the self, at the high price of dehumanization. What Sublime can compensate for violence against the self?

Blinded Oedipus is equivalent to the crippled smith-god, Vulcan or Thor or Urthona, for blinding or crippling alike are castrating movements that hold back from the full impairment of the imagining faculty. *Daemonization,* as a revisionary ratio, is a self-crippling act, intended to purchase knowledge by a playing at the loss of power, but more frequently resulting in a true loss of the powers of making. It is a false Dionysiac gesture that reduces the precursor's human glory by handing back all his hard-won victories to the daemonic world. So Nietzsche told us, in his backward critical glance at *The Birth of Tragedy,* when he rejected his youthful vision of a world "made to appear, at every instant, as a successful *solution* of God's own tensions, as an ever new vision projected by that grand sufferer for whom illusion is the only possible mode of redemption."

Freud humanely saw the Oedipus complex as only a phase in the development of character, to be superseded by the *überich* (superego) as mock-rational censor. Yet no poet-as-poet completes such a development and still remains a poet. In the imagination, the Oedipal phase *develops backwards,* to enrich and make yet more inchoate the id. The formula of *daemonization* is: "Where my poetic father's *I* was, there *it* shall be," or even better, "there my *I* is, more closely mixed with *it.*" This is Romanticism as a study of the nostalgias, the primitivizing dream of so many gloriously estranged sensibilities. To *daemonize* is to reach that antecedent stage of psychic organization where everything passional is ambivalent, yet to reach it with the difference that makes a poem possible, the willed perverseness of a double consciousness wholly centered on the poetic survival value of malforming all that is past.

Nothing could be further from spontaneous aggression than what I am terming *daemonization,* and yet they look suspiciously alike. So many songs of triumph, read close, begin to appear rituals of separation, that a wary reader may wonder if the truly strong poet ever has any antagonist beyond the self and its strongest precursor. Here is Collins, invoking Fear, yet what has he to fear except himself and John Milton?

> Thou, to whom the world unknown,
>   With all its shadowy shapes, is shown;
>   Who seest, appalled, the unreal scene,
> While fancy lifts the veil between:
>   Ah fear! ah frantic fear!
>   I see, I see thee near.
>   . . . .
>   . . . .
> Wrapt in thy cloudy veil, the incestuous queen
>   Sighed the sad call her son and husband heard,
> When once alone it broke the silent scene,
>   And he, the wretch of Thebes, no more appeared.
>   . . . .

. . . .
Dark power, with shuddering meek submitted thought,
Be mine to read the visions old
Which thy awakening bards have told:
And, lest thou meet my blasted view,
Hold each strange tale devoutly true. . . .

Here Fear is Collins' own daemon (as Fletcher observes), the more-than-poetic madness that beckons him into the upward fall of Extravagance. Confronting the daemonic, Collins wavers between Oedipus the seer and blinded Oedipus, using the language and rhythms of Milton's *Penseroso* to *daemonize* the precursor, to locate Milton's baneful beauty where only *it,* the id, can dwell. Yet at how high a price Collins purchases this indefinite rapture, this cloudy Sublime! For his poem is one with his deepest repression of his own humanity, and accurately prophesies the terrible pathos of his fate, to make us remember him always, with all his gifts, as Dr. Johnson's "Poor Collins."

Most of what we have called the madness or "perilous balance" of the Bards of Sensibility was simply their exercise of this dangerous defense, the revisionary ratio of *daemonization.* The natural history of Sensibility reduces to the willful misprision of a too-consciously post-Miltonic poetry. So much of the mid-eighteenth-century Sublime is subsumed by this anxiety of influence that we must wonder whether the revived Sublime was ever more than a compound of repression and the perverse celebration of loss, as though less could become more, through a continuity of regressiveness and self-deception. Yet more than the Sublime transport of Thomson, Collins, Cowper is placed in jeopardy by our gathering awareness. What of Blake's Counter-Sublime, and Wordsworth's? Is all the *ekstasis,* the final step beyond, of Romantic vision only an intensity of repression previously unmatched in the history of the imagination? Is Romanticism after all only the waning out of the Enlightenment, and its prophetic poetry only an illusory therapy, not so much a saving fiction as an unconscious lie against the difficult human effort of holding the middle ground between instinctual existence and all morality?

If there are answers to these questions, they will not be less dialectical than the questions themselves, or than the Idiot Questioner within us that silently plots all such questions as a pragmatic malevolence. Better to remember the vision of our father Abraham, when "an horror of great darkness fell upon him," and what the most poignant of the poets of Sensibility was compelled to make out of it. "And it came to pass, that, when the sun went down, and it was dark, behold a smoking furnace, and a burning lamp that passed between those pieces." Christopher Smart, in his darkness, first cried out: "For the furnace itself shall come up at the last according to Abraham's vision," and then added, stung by the repressiveness of the Covering Cherub, a more prayerful prophecy: "For SHADOW is a fair Word from God, which is not returnable till the furnace comes up."

Five

Heaven bestows light and influence on this lower world, which reflects the blessed rays, though it cannot recompence them. So man may make a return to God, but no requital.

COLERIDGE

Askesis

or PURGATION AND SOLIPSISM

The Prometheus in every strong poet incurs the guilt of having devoured just that portion of the infant Dionysus contained in the precursor poet. Orphism, for latecomers, reduces to a variety of sublimation, the truest of defenses against the anxiety of influence, and the one most impairing to the poetic self. Hence Nietzsche, lovingly recognizing in Socrates the first master of sublimation, found in Socrates also the destroyer of tragedy. Had he lived to read Freud, Nietzsche might somewhat admiringly have seen in him another Socrates, come to revive the primary vision of a rational substitute for the unattainable, antithetical gratifications of life and art alike.

Whether sublimation of sexual instincts plays a central part in the genesis of poetry is hardly relevant to the reading of poetry, and has no part in the dialectic of misprision. But sublimation of aggressive instincts is central to writing and reading poetry, and this is almost identical with the total process of poetic misprision. Poetic sublimation is an *askesis,* a way of purgation intending a state of solitude as its proximate goal. Intoxicated by the fresh repressive force of a personalized Counter-Sublime, the strong poet in his daemonic elevation is empowered to turn his energy upon himself, and achieves, at terrible cost, his clearest victory in wrestling with the mighty dead.

Fenichel, faithful to the Founder's spirit, almost sings a paean to the splendors of sublimation. For, in Freud's vision, only sublimation can give us a kind of thinking liberated from its own sexual past, and again only sublimation can modify an instinctive impulse without destroying it. Poets in particular, as Nietzsche might have remarked, are as poets incapable of existing either with prolonged frustration or with stoical renunciation. How can they give pleasure, if in no way they have received it? But how can they receive the deepest pleasure, the ecstasy of priority, of self-begetting, of an assured autonomy, if their way to the True Subject and their own True Selves lies through the precursor's subject and his self?

Kierkegaard, in so unfavorably contrasting Orpheus to Abraham, followed Plato's *Symposium,* where the poet-of-poets is condemned for his softness, which appears to mean his incapacity for sublimation. And truly, it would seem odd to cite Orpheus as an exemplar of the ascetic spirit. Yet Orphism, the natural religion of all poets as poets, offered itself as an *askesis.* The Orphics, who worshipped Time as the origin of all things, nevertheless reserved their true devotion for Dionysus, devoured by the Titans but reborn from Semele. This myth's sorrow is that man, rising from the ashes of the sinful Titans, has in him the evil Prometheanism and the good Dionysian element. All poetic ecstasy, all sense that the poet steps out from man into god, reduces to this sour myth, as does all poetic asceticism, which begins as the dark doctrine of metempsychosis and its attendant fears of devouring a former version of the self.

The ephebe, transforming himself through the purgations of his revisionary stance, is the direct descendant of every Orphic adept who rolled himself in mud and meal that he might be raised out of the fury and the mire of being merely human. Doom, for the Orphic, was to fall victim to repetition compulsion, and so to carry water in a sieve in Hades. Every hateful exclusiveness ever felt by a Western poet is ultimately Orphic in its origin, but so is every poetic Sublime from Pindar to the present. The nausea of the poetic sufferer is indistinguishable from his sublimity, *to him,* but few readers are as antithetical as their poets, those liberating gods whose nostalgia is more pungent than their divinity. Nietzsche was a master psychologist in seeing that poets are far more intense in their Dionysian self-deception than in their share of our common Promethean guilt.

A philosophy of composition (not of psychogenesis) is a genealogy of imagination necessarily, a study of the only guilt that matters to a poet, the guilt of indebtedness. Nietzsche is the true psychologist of this guilt, which may be at the center of his concern with the will—not so much the will to power as a counter-will that rises in him, seeking not strength but the disinterestedness that his master Schopenhauer had sought. Nietzsche, though he had transvalued disinterestedness, remained haunted by it.

"There is perhaps nothing more terrible in man's earliest history than his mnemotechnics," Nietzsche remarked, for his insight associated every creation of a memory with hideous pain. Every custom (including, we may surmise, poetic tradition) "is a sequence of . . . processes of appropriation, including the resistances used in each instance, the attempted transformations for purposes of defense or reaction, as well as the results of successful counterattacks." In *The Genealogy of Morals,* the sickness of bad conscience is diagnosed as necessary, and at last as a phase in the human creation of gods. Vico's "severe poem" of our imaginative origins is gentle when contrasted to Nietzsche's terrible vision of "the relationship between living men and their forebears." The sacrifices and achievements of the ancestors are sole guarantee for the survival of early societies, who need to repay the dead:

> . . . the fear of the ancestor and his power and the consciousness of indebtedness increase in direct proportion as the power of the tribe itself increases, as it becomes more successful . . . we arrive at a situation in which the ancestors of the most powerful tribes have become so fearful to the imagination that they have receded at last into a numinous shadow: the ancestor becomes a god.

Part of the repayment to the numinous shadow, Nietzsche insisted, was the ascetic ideal, which in artists meant "nothing or too many things." Against the ascetic ideal, Nietzsche set the "antithetical ideal," and asked desperately: "Where do we find an antithetical will enforcing an antithetical ideal?" Part of the answer Yeats sought to embody from *Per Amica Silentia Lunae* on in his life's work, and perhaps Yeats gave a fuller answer (for all its incompleteness) than any other post-Nietzschean artist, until at last a curiously inverted vision of the ascetic ideal came to mar his *Last Poems and Plays.*

It is not particularly pleasant to regard poetry, at its strongest, as the successful sublimation of our instinctual aggressiveness, much as though a Pindaric ode were of one family with the triumph-songs of the geese described by Lorenz. But what the poets call their Purgatory is largely what Platonists, Christians, Nietzscheans, or Freudians would agree to call a kind of sublimation, or ego defenses that work. As the Freudian account of sublimation is the most amiably reductive, we can profit by following it here. The mechanisms of defense in sublimation are varied: changes from passivity to activity, direct confrontation of the dangerous forces or impulses, the conversion of the forces to their opposite. To cite Fenichel: "In sublimation, the original impulse vanishes because its energy is withdrawn in favor of the cathexis of its substitute." Libido flows on, undisturbed, but is desexualized, and destructive tendencies are drained off from the aggressive influx of our energies and desires.

Freud, in *The Ego and the Id,* speculated that sublimation was closely related to identification, an identification itself reliant upon distortion of aim or object, which may go so far as transformation into the opposite. If we convert this speculation into the context of our typology of evasions, then sublimation becomes a form of *askesis,* a self-curtailment which seeks transformation at the expense of narrowing the creative circumference of precursor and ephebe alike. The final product of the process of poetic *askesis* is the formation of an imaginative equivalent of the superego, a fully developed *poetic will,* harsher than conscience, and so the Urizen in each strong poet, his maturely internalized aggressiveness.

Lou Andreas-Salomé, whom we remember as the beloved of Nietzsche and Rilke and also as Freud's disciple, followed another of her celebrated lovers, the melancholy Tausk, when she observed that sublimation was actually our own self-realization and might better be called "elaboration." Elaborating ourselves, we become both Prometheus and Narcissus; or rather, only the truly strong poet can go on being both, making his culture, and raptly contemplating his own central place in it. But for this contemplation, he must make a sacrifice, as every creation-by-evasion, every latecomer's making, depends upon sacrifice.

Cornford, in his *Principium Sapientiae,* remarks the curiosity "that in Hesiod mankind first appears in connexion with the sacrifice, when Prometheus cheated Zeus of the better portion, as if sacrifice to the gods were, as in the Babylonian doctrine, man's primary function. In Genesis also the first sin committed after the expulsion of our first parents from Eden was occasioned by the sacrifices offered by Abel and Cain." Cornford concludes that all sacrifice is done to renew human vitality. In the process of poetic misprision, sacrifice diminishes human vitality, for here less is more. Though we have idealized Western poetry almost since its origins (following in this the poets themselves, who knew better), the writing (and reading) of poems is a sacrificial process, a purgation that drains more than it replenishes. Each poem is an evasion not only of another poem, but also of itself, which is to say that every poem is a misinterpretation of what it might have been.

The gods cannot be bribed, Plato said, and so sacrifice could not give gratitude for gifts supposedly to come. The *Phaedo* proposes a truer catharsis for the philosophic soul: "Purification . . . consists in separating the soul as much as possible from the body . . . and concentrating itself by itself." Such radical dualism cannot be the *askesis* of the poetic soul, where separation must take place within the soul itself. Internalization is the poet's way of separation. The soul's estrangement from itself is not intended, yet follows from the attempt at estranging not only all precursors, but their worlds, which means to have estranged poetry itself. Error about life is necessary for life, and error about poetry is necessary for poetry.

Poetic *askesis* begins at the heights of the Counter-Sublime, and compensates for the poet's involuntary shock at his own daemonic expansiveness. Without *askesis,* the strong poet, like Stevens, is fated to become the rabbit as king of the ghosts:

The grass is full

And full of yourself. The trees around are for you,
The whole of the wideness of night is for you,
A self that touches all edges,

You become a self that fills the four corners of night.

Humped high, humped up, the poet will become a carving in space unless he can wound himself *without further emptying himself of his inspiration.* He cannot afford another *kenosis.* Useful surrender, for him, is now a curtailment, a sacrifice of some part of himself whose absence will individuate him more, as a poet. *Askesis,* as a successful defense against the anxiety of influence, posits a new kind of reduction in the poetic self, most generally expressed as a purgatorial blinding or at least a veiling. The realities of other selves and of all that is external are diminished alike, until a new style of harshness emerges, whose rhetorical emphasis can be read off as one degree of solipsism or another.

What the strong poet, like the solipsist, *means* is right, for this egocentricity is itself a major training in imagination. Purgatory for post-Enlightenment strong poets is always oxymoronic, and never merely painful, because every narrowing of circumference is compensated for by the poetic illusion (a delusion, and yet a strong poem) that the center therefore will hold better. What Coleridge (as philosopher, not as poet) called "outness," the theocentric sanctioning of externals and of others, is of no interest to the strong poet as poet. I am making the suggestion (which I myself dislike) that in his purgatorial *askesis* the strong poet knows only himself and the Other he must at last destroy, his precursor, who may well (by now) be an imaginary or composite figure, yet who remains formed by actual past poems that will not allow themselves to be forgotten. For *clinamen* and *tessera* strive to correct or complete the dead, and *kenosis* and *daemonization* work to repress memory of the dead, but *askesis* is the contest proper, the match-to-the-death with the dead.

Yet, if we historicized any account that theorized sublimation, what else could we hope to find but a struggle with all our ancestors? If all self-development is a sublimation, and so merely an elaboration, how endlessly can we desire the elaboration to proceed, how much elaboration can we bear? Pragmatically, we want as much as will not upset the ideas-of-order that keep us going, but we after all (myself and those for whom I write) are not poets, but readers. Can the truly strong poet bear only to be an elaboration of the poet who forever holds priority over him?

Yet there was a great age before the Flood, when influence was generous (or poets in their innermost natures thought it so), an age that goes all the way from Homer to Shakespeare. At the heart of this matrix of generous influence is Dante and his relation to his precursor Virgil, who moved his ephebe only to love and emulation and not to anxiety. Yes, but though no Shadow falls between Virgil and Dante, something else stands in its place. John Freccero beautifully illuminates this great sublimation, an ancestor of every subsequent *askesis* undergone by the strong poet:

In the *Purgatorio,* XXVII, the pilgrim & Statius & Virgil cross through the wall of fire, are met by the angel and all the traditional trappings are there, including lots of father & son talk. Walls, barriers, echoes of all of the ancient and medieval themes you could imagine. This is also the point at which Virgil disappears from the poem and is replaced by Beatrice. What is not generally recognized, however, is that it is also the point at which the greatest number of Virgilian echoes appear, including the only direct quotation of Virgil in the poem (in Latin), all of them deliberately skewed: First, the words of Dido, when she sees Aeneas and recalls the ancient passion that bound her to her husband and so foresees her own death on the pyre: *"agnosco veteris flammae vestigia."* In the *Purgatorio* Dante uses the line to recall his first passion for Beatrice, as she returns: *"conosco i signi dell'antica fiamma."* Second, the angels sing, to greet Beatrice: *"Manibus o date lilia plenis. . . ."* This is the line used by Anchises to point out the shade of the prematurely dead son of Augustus in the *"Tu Marcellus eris"* passage marking the ultimate *échec* in spite of the eternity of Rome. Scholars say that what is meant is purple lilies of mourning. The implication in *Purgatorio* is obviously the white lilies of the Resurrection. The pilgrim turns to Virgil for help in the face of the momentous return and finds the *dolce padre* gone: *"Virgilio, Virgilio, Virgilio,"* echoing Virgil's own confession of the impotence of poetry in the story of Orpheus in IV *Georgic: "Eurydice, Eurydice, Eurydice."* So the dark eros of Dido is transformed by the retrospective redemption of Beatrice's return, the eternity in the political order is at last matched by personal immortality of the resurrection, poetry becomes stronger than Death and for the first time in the poem, the Pilgrim is named as Beatrice calls him: *"Dante!"*

—from a letter to the author

This naming-after-purgation is, however, the last element here that remains ancestral, for every post-enlightenment master moves, not towards a sharing-with-others as Dante does after this great moment, but towards a being-with-oneself. *Askesis* in Wordsworth, Keats, Browning, Whitman, Yeats, and Stevens, to examine a half-dozen representative modern figures, is necessarily a revisionary ratio that concludes on the border of solipsism. I shall take these examples by pairs—Wordsworth and Keats, Browning and Yeats, Whitman and Stevens, for in each case the earlier figure is both a precursor and a sharer in a common precursor: respectively Milton, Shelley, Emerson.

Here is Wordsworth, in the grand fragment *Home at Grasmere:*

> While yet an innocent little one, with a heart
> That doubtless wanted not its tender moods,
> I breathed (for this I better recollect)
> Among wild appetites and blind desires,
> Motions of savage instinct my delight
> And exaltation. Nothing at that time
> So welcome, no temptation half so dear
> As that which urged me to a daring feat,
> Deep pools, tall trees, black chasm, and dizzy crags,
> And tottering towers: I loved to stand and read
> Their looks forbidding, read and disobey,
> Sometimes in act and evermore in thought.
> With impulses, that scarcely were by these
> Surpassed in strength, I heard of danger met
> Or sought with courage; enterprise forlorn
> By one, sole keeper of his own intent,
> Or by a resolute few, who for the sake
> Of glory fronted multitudes in arms.
> Yea, to this hour I cannot read a Tale
> Of two brave vessels matched in deadly fight,
> And fighting to the death, but I am pleased
> More than a wise man ought to be; I wish,
> Fret, burn, and struggle, and in soul am there.
> But me hath Nature tamed, and bade to seek
> For other agitations, or be calm;
> Hath dealt with me as with a turbulent stream,
> Some nursling of the mountains which she leads
> Through quiet meadows, after he has learnt
> His strength, and had his triumph and his joy,
> His desperate course of tumult and of glee.
> That which in stealth by Nature was performed
> Hath Reason sanctioned: her deliberate Voice
> Hath said; be mild, and cleave to gentle things,
> Thy glory and thy happiness be there.
> Nor fear, though thou confide in me, a want

Of aspirations that have been—of foes
To wrestle with, and victory to complete,
Bounds to be leapt, darkness to be explored;
All that inflamed thy infant heart, the love,
The longing, the contempt, the undaunted quest,
All shall survive, though changed their office, all
Shall live, it is not in their power to die.
Then farewell to the Warrior's Schemes, farewell
The forwardness of soul which looks that way
Upon a less incitement than the Cause
Of Liberty endangered, and farewell
That other hope, long mine, the hope to fill
The heroic trumpet with the Muse's breath!

This *askesis* yields up a Wordsworth who might have
been a greater poet than the one he became, a more exter-
nalized maker who would have had a subject beyond that
of his own subjectivity. An enormous curtailment made
Wordsworth the inventor of modern poetry, which at last
we can recognize as the diminished thing it is, or more
plainly: modern poetry (Romanticism) is the result of a
more prodigious sublimation of imagination than West-
ern poetry from Homer through Milton had to undergo.
Wordsworth is in the unhappy position of *celebrating* not
a mere desexualization but a genuine loss of "All that in-
flamed thy infant heart, the love,/The longing, the con-
tempt, the undaunted quest." His faith is that all these
"shall survive, though changed their office, all/Shall live,"
but soon enough his poetry will not sustain such a faith.
   In *Home at Grasmere,* the expected recompense for this
sublimation is attempted immediately, in the next and
concluding passage of the fragment, which became the cel-
ebrated "Prospectus" to *The Excursion.* Here the *askesis*
is revealed in its complete circumference, as much a re-
duction of Milton as it is of Wordsworth. And here too,

Wordsworth's deepest obsession as a monstrously strong poet is revealed:

> . . . that my Song
> With star-like virtue in its place may shine,
> Shedding benignant influence, and secure
> Itself from all malevolent effect
> Of those mutations that extend their sway
> Throughout the nether sphere!

In a sonnet written two years later, addressed to Milton, the precursor is described as Wordsworth sees himself here:

> Thy soul was like a Star, and dwelt apart:
> Thou hadst a voice whose sound was like the sea;
> Pure as the naked heavens, majestic, free. . . .

The prayer then is to be an influence, and not to be influenced, and the precursor is praised for having been *what one has become*. One's own pure isolation is now Milton's isolation also, and having overcome Milton, one asserts that one has overcome oneself. Wordsworth, whose art depends upon persuading the reader that relationship with external selves and landscapes is still possible, is an immense master at estranging other selves and every landscape *from himself*. This healer heals only the wounds he himself inflicts.

Keats, less than twenty years later, struggles with a purgatorial burden remarkably similar, the need to sublimate by internalizing "the undaunted quest" that could still allow Milton a vision of War in Heaven. But the Keatsian *askesis* is more drastic, for his Covering Cherub is a double form, Milton *and* Wordsworth. In Keats, the purgation becomes wholly explicit, and is the kernel of *The Fall of Hyperion*, where his Muse Moneta confronts the poet:

. . . "If thou canst not ascend
These steps, die on that marble where thou art.
Thy flesh, near cousin to the common dust,
Will parch for lack of nutriment,—thy bones
Will wither in few years, and vanish so
That not the quickest eye could find a grain
Of what thou now art on that pavement cold.
The sands of thy short life are spent this hour,
And no hand in the universe can turn
Thy hourglass, if these gummed leaves be burnt
Ere thou canst mount up these immortal steps."
I heard, I look'd: two senses both at once,
So fine, so subtle, felt the tyranny
Of that fierce threat and the hard task proposed.
Prodigious seem'd the toil; the leaves were yet
Burning,—when suddenly a palsied chill
Struck from the paved level up my limbs,
And was ascending quick to put cold grasp
Upon those streams that pulse beside the throat!
I shriek'd, and the sharp anguish of my shriek
Stung my own ears—I strove hard to escape
The numbness, strove to gain the lowest step.
Slow, heavy, deadly was my pace: the cold
Grew stifling, suffocating, at the heart;
And when I clasp'd my hands I felt them not.
One minute before death, my iced foot touch'd
The lowest stair; and, as it touch'd, life seem'd
To pour in at the toes. . . .

What is sublimated here is the most integral instance of a sensuous imagination since Shakespeare's. And what ends here is Keats's poetry, though the poet lived on for a year and several months after giving up this major fragment. Surely his mortal illness is the base from which this vision rises, but we need to ask: poetically, what is the numbness that nearly destroys Keats here? The *askesis* here is not *of* the senses, but of Keats's *faith in* them, a faith so sublime as to be unmatchable in humanistic poetry. Yet this faith, though rooted in Keats's temperament, came to him from the young Milton, with his unitary dream of human possibilities, a last sublimity of the Renaissance, and from the young Wordsworth, visionary of the Revolution. If Keats purges it from himself, he purges it also from the earlier splendors of his Great Originals. As matured (or ruined) men, they underwent their own purgations but left their earlier visions extant. Keats does for them what they could not bear to do for themselves: he questions the deepest and most moving naturalistic illusions that the spirit ever generated. And having questioned these, and his own best self with them, he is granted a last vision of himself, but in the splendor of an ultimate isolation:

> Without stay or prop,
> But my own weak mortality, I bore
> The load of this eternal quietude. . . .

The hardness of style, the inevitability of phrasing of *The Fall of Hyperion,* stem from the Keatsian version of *askesis,* a humanization that almost redeems this bitter ratio of revision. With poets less balanced, there is no redemption. Browning and Yeats, both dependent heirs of Shelley (with Browning also, by Yeats's confession, a "dangerous influence" upon him), perform a massive self-curtailment in their full maturity as poets. Browning's sublimation gave him his kind of dramatic monologue, and with it the art of nightmare, unmatched in English:

> **xxv**
> Then came a bit of stubbed ground, once a wood,
>   Next a marsh, it would seem, and now mere earth
>   Desperate and done with; (so a fool finds mirth,
> Makes a thing and then mars it, till his mood

Changes and off he goes!) within a rood—
   Bog, clay and rubble, sand and stark black dearth.

XXVI

Now blotches rankling, coloured gay and grim,
   Now patches where some leanness of the soil's
   Broke into moss or substances like boils;
Then came some palsied oak, a cleft in him
Like a distorted mouth that splits its rim
   Gaping at death, and dies while it recoils.

XXVII

And just as far as ever from the end!
   Nought in the distance but the evening, nought
   To point my footstep further! At the thought,
A great black bird, Apollyon's bosom-friend,
Sailed past, nor beat his wide wing dragon-penned
   That brushed my cap—perchance the guide I sought.

XXVIII

For, looking up, aware I somehow grew
   'Spite of the dusk, the plain had given place
   All round to mountains—with such name to grace
Mere ugly heights and heaps now stolen in view.
How thus they had surprised me,—solve it, you!
   How to get from them was no clearer case.

XXIX

Yet half I seemed to recognize some trick
   Of mischief happened to me, God knows when—
   In a bad dream perhaps. Here ended, then,
Progress this way. When, in the very nick
Of giving up, one time more, came a click
   As when a trap shuts—you're inside the den!

XXX

Burningly it came on me all at once,
   This was the place! those two hills on the right,
   Crouched like two bulls locked horn in horn in fight;
While to the left, a tall scalped mountain . . . Dunce,

Dotard, a-dozing at the very nonce,
    After a life spent training for the sight!

XXXI

What in the midst lay but the Tower itself?
    The round squat turret, blind as the fool's heart,
    Built of brown stone, without a counterpart
In the whole world. The tempest's mocking elf
Points to the shipman thus the unseen shelf
    He strikes on, only when the timbers start.

Why call this the consequence of an *askesis?* Or why find the same cause for Yeats's *Cuchulain Comforted,* where the hero accepts the community of cowards as his rightful place in the afterlife? "A poet and not an honest man" is the whole of an aphorism by Pascal. To revise the precursor is to lie, not against being, but against time, and *askesis* is peculiarly a lie against the truth of time, the time in which the ephebe hoped to attain an autonomy already tainted by time, ravaged by otherness.

Shelley initially converted both Browning and Yeats to poetry by giving them an exemplar of self-consuming autonomy, of the only quest that could bring them the hope of re-begetting themselves. Both of them were to be haunted by the moral prophecy of the *Defence,* where Shelley says of the poets, however erring as men, that "they have been washed in the blood of the mediator and redeemer, Time." This is Orphic faith, and in its purity neither Browning nor Yeats was strong enough to live and die. Shelley's Orpheus is the Poet of *Alastor,* who beholds the departure of Vision and Love, and cries aloud: "Sleep and death/Shall not divide us long!" From this remorselessness of shattered quest, Browning and Yeats had to rescue themselves, as sons of a poetic father whose imaginative purity no descendant could bear to sustain.

When Childe Roland fails to recognize the Dark Tower

until it is upon him, despite a lifetime's preparation, or when Cuchulain is content to sew a shroud, and then to sing in chorus with his opposites, convicted cowards and traitors all (like Roland's lost companions of the quest), we are given radical emblems of *askesis,* and of its terrible cost to the sons of too incorruptible an imaginative hero. What is most terrifying about Shelley is his Orphic integrity, the swiftness of a spirit too impatient for the compromises without which societal existence and even natural life are just not possible. Browning's immersion in the grotesque and Yeats's addiction to brutality are both sublimations of their precursor's quasi-divine heroism, his astonishing aberration with the Absolute. But in these curtailments, as opposed to the sublimations of greater figures like Wordsworth and Keats, we have more difficulty in seeing that there was loss nearly as large as the so much more palpable gain.

Freud's notion of sublimation is quantitative, and implies always an upper limit beyond which instinctual impulses rebel. Poetic *askesis,* as a revisionary ratio, is also quantitative, for the Purgatory of poets is rarely a very populated place. The poet and his Muse are inhabitants enough, and frequently the Muse is missing. Childe Roland and Cuchulain, heroic questers who can know defeat only through its antinomies, are alone except for their little bands of failures, traitors and cowards whose presence testifies to all that is most equivocal in the fearful strength of the heroes themselves. But the difference between Childe Roland and his precursors, between Cuchulain and his comforters, is that only the hero's purgation is an *askesis,* a road through to freedom that is significant act.

Browning's monologue, like Yeats's visionary lyric, is an evasion, and hence a curtailment of Orphic poetry, the Shelleyan trumpet of a prophecy. *Askesis* in strong American poets emphasizes the goal of the process, self-sustain-ing solitude, rather than the process itself. Milton and Wordsworth, whose mutual influence created the ethos of post-Enlightenment English poetry, both accommodated their fearful strength to the necessities of sublimation, but the Great Original of a genuinely American poetry would not. In Emerson, the power of the mind and the power of the eye endeavor to become one, which makes *askesis* impossible:

> As, in the sun, objects paint their images on the retina of the eye, so they, sharing the aspiration of the whole universe, tend to paint a far more delicate copy of their essence in his mind. Like the metamorphosis of things into higher organic forms is their change into melodies. Over everything stands its daemon or soul, and, as the form of the thing is reflected by the eye, so the soul of the thing is reflected by a melody. The sea, the mountain-ridge, Niagara, and every flower-bed, pre-exist, or super-exist, in precantations, which sail like odors in the air, and when any man goes by with an ear sufficiently fine, he overhears them and endeavors to write down the notes without diluting or depraving them. . . . This insight, which expresses itself by what is called Imagination, is a very high sort of seeing, which does not come by study, but by the intellect being where and what it sees; by sharing the path or circuit of things through forms, and so making them translucid to others.

This is the American Sublime, which will not surrender the pleasure principle to the reality principle, even in the expectation that deferred fulfillment will protect the pleasure principle. The eye, most tyrannous of the bodily senses, from which nature freed Milton, and from which Wordsworth freed nature, is in American poetry a rage and a program. Where the eye dominates, without curtailment, *askesis* tends to center on the self's awareness of other selves. The solipsism of our major poets—Emerson,

Whitman, Dickinson, Frost, Stevens, Crane—is augmented because the eye declines to be purged. Reality reduces to the Emersonian Me and the Not-Me (my body and nature), and excludes all others, except insofar as the precursors have become inescapable components of the Me.

Whitman, in *Crossing Brooklyn Ferry,* sees "the sunset, the pouring-in of the flood-tide, the falling-back to the sea of the ebb-tide," and is comforted that others coming after him will see as and what he does. But his majestic poem, like all his wholly realized works, is centered only on his isolate self, and on Emersonian seeing, which is not far from shamanistic practice, and has little to do with observation of externals. In Whitman, the Emersonian isolation deepens, the eye becomes even more tyrannical, and as the eye's power identifies with the sun, an immense *askesis* is accomplished:

> Dazzling and tremendous how quick the sun-rise
>   would kill me
> If I could not now and always send sun-rise out of me.

> We also ascend dazzling and tremendous as the sun,
> We found our own O my soul in the calm and cool
>   of the daybreak.

> My voice goes after what my eyes cannot reach,
> With the twirl of my tongue I encompass worlds and
>   volumes of worlds.

Why call this limitless expansiveness an *askesis?* In this enormous elaboration of Emerson, what is being offered up for sublimation? What curtailment makes of Whitman this voice that sees what even his sight cannot reach? If nothing is got for nothing, as Emersonian Compensation insisted, for what loss is the Emersonian bard compensated in this solipsistic sunrise? The loss is what Emerson called "a great Defeat" (of which Christ was an example), and Emerson added: "we demand victory." Christ "did well. . . . But he that shall come shall do better. The mind requires a far higher exhibition of character, one which shall make itself good to the senses as well as to the soul; a success to the senses as well as to the soul." Whitman's incarnation as the sun is an Emersonian great Defeat, a flowing-in that contains an ebbing-out, an *askesis* of the Emersonian prophecy of the Central Bard who shall come:

In the far South the sun of autumn is passing
Like Walt Whitman walking along a ruddy shore.
He is singing and chanting the things that are part of him,
The worlds that were and will be, death and day.
Nothing is final, he chants. No man shall see the end.
His beard is of fire and his staff is a leaping flame.

A discussion of poetic *askesis* must come at last to Stevens, whose work is dominated by that revisionary ratio. Stevens, who had "a passion for yes," resisted his own rigorous sublimations. He regrets not being "A more severe,/More harassing master," yet he was anything but an ascetic of the spirit, and would have been happy to make poems even more like pineapples. The primary passion in him is the Orphic aspiration of Emerson and Whitman, the quest for an American Sublime, but the anxiety of influence malformed this passion, and Stevens consequently developed a tendency to speak more reductively than he himself could bear to accept. At his best, Stevens labored to "make the visible a little hard/To see," in defiance of his own tradition, but throughout his poetry the purgation-by-solitude reaches after an amplitude unknown even in Emerson, Whitman, and Dickinson. "Freud's eye," Stevens wrote, "was the microscope of potency," and Stevens, more than any modern poet, composed naturally out of the state of being Psychological Man. Sublimation in Stevens is a curtailment of a Keatsian sensibility, of a mind that has obeyed Moneta's injunction to "think of the earth" only to discover that such thought does not suffice:

> Nothing could be more hushed than the way
> The moon moves toward the night.
> But what his mother was returns and cries on his breast.
>
> The red ripeness of round leaves is thick
> With the spices of red summer,
> But she that he loved turns cold at his light touch.
>
> What good is it that the earth is justified,
> That it is complete, that it is an end,
> That in itself it is enough?

In Stevens, the reader confronts an *askesis* of the entire Romantic tradition, of Wordsworth as much as Keats, Emerson as well as Whitman. No modern poet half so strong as Stevens chose so large a self-curtailment, sacrificed so much instinctual impulse in the name of being a latecomer. Freud, revising himself, at last concluded that it was anxiety that produced repression and not repression that produced anxiety, a realization everywhere exemplified by Stevens' poetry. Imaginatively Stevens knew that both ego and id are organized systems, and even organized against one another, but perhaps Stevens was better off not knowing that his ego anxieties about priority and originality were provoked perpetually by his id's absorption of his precursors, who therefore operated in him not as censorious powers, but almost as varieties of the instinctual life. A Romantic humanist thus by temperament, but a reductive ironist in his anxieties, Stevens became an astonishing blend of poetic strains, foreign and native. He demonstrates that the strongest modern poetry is created by *askesis,* but leaves us sorrowful for the curtailment of what he might have done, if free of the terrible necessities of misprision, as here of Emerson:

> The afternoon is visibly a source,
> Too wide, too irised, to be more than calm,
>
> Too much like thinking to be less than thought,
> Obscurest parent, obscurest patriarch,
> A daily majesty of meditation,
>
> That comes and goes in silences of its own,
> We think, then, as the sun shines or does not.
> We think as wind skitters on a pond in a field
>
> Or we put mantles on our words because
> The same wind, rising and rising, makes a sound
> Like the last muting of winter as it ends.
>
> A new scholar replacing an older one reflects
> A moment on this fantasia. He seeks
> For a human that can be accounted for.

The search for a human that can be accounted for, a search that is a diminishment of the larger Emersonian dream, threatens also to be not what Emerson called a great Defeat, but the kind of defeat appropriate to the ascetic spirit, or a defeat of poetry itself.

Six

No anchorage is.
Sleep is not, death is not;
Who seem to die live.

EMERSON

Apophrades

or THE RETURN OF THE DEAD

Empedocles held that our psyche at death returned to the fire whence it came. But our daemon, at once our guilt and our ever-potential divinity, came to us not from the fire but from our precursors. The stolen element had to be returned; the daemon was never stolen but inherited, and at death was passed on to the ephebe, the latecomer who could accept both the crime and the godhood at once.

The genealogy of imagination traces the descent of the daemon, and never of the psyche, but analogues abound between these descents:

> It may be that one life is a punishment
> For another, as the son's life for the father's.

It may be that one strong poet's work expiates for the work of a precursor. It seems more likely that later visions cleanse themselves at the expense of earlier ones. But the strong dead return, in poems as in our lives, and they do not come back without darkening the living. The wholly mature strong poet is peculiarly vulnerable to this last phase of his revisionary relationship to the dead. This vulnerability is most evident in poems that quest for a final clarity, that seek to be definitive statements, testaments to what is uniquely the strong poet's gift (or what he wishes us to remember as his unique gift):

> I arose, and for a space
> The scene of woods and waters seemed to keep,
>
> Though it was now broad day, a gentle trace
> Of light diviner than the common sun
> Sheds on the common earth, and all the place
>
> Was filled with magic sounds woven into one
> Oblivious melody, confusing sense. . . .

Here, at his end, Shelley is open again to the terror of Wordsworth's "Intimations" ode, and yields to his precursor's "light of common day":

> —I among the multitude
> Was swept—me, sweetest flowers·delayed not long;
> Me, not the shadow nor the solitude,
>
> Me, not that falling stream's Lethean song;
> Me, not the phantom of that early Form
> Which moved upon its motion—but among
>
> The thickest billows of that living storm
> I plunged, and bared my bosom to the clime
> Of that cold light, whose airs too soon deform.

By 1822, when Shelley experienced this last vision, the poet Wordsworth was long dead (though the man Wordsworth survived Shelley by twenty-eight years, until 1850). But strong poets keep returning from the dead, and only through the quasi-willing mediumship of other strong poets. *How* they return is the decisive matter, for if they return intact, then the return impoverishes the later poets, dooming them to be remembered—if at all—as having ended in poverty, in an imaginative need they could not themselves gratify.

The *apophrades,* the dismal or unlucky days upon which the dead return to inhabit their former houses, come to the strongest poets, but with the very strongest there is a grand and final revisionary movement that purifies even this last influx. Yeats and Stevens, the strongest poets of our century, and Browning and Dickinson, the strongest of the later nineteenth century, can give us vivid instances of this most cunning of revisionary ratios. For all of them achieve a style that captures and oddly retains priority over their precursors, so that the tyranny of time almost is overturned, and one can believe, for startled moments, that they are being *imitated by their ancestors.*

In this observation, I want to distinguish the phenomenon from the witty insight of Borges, that artists *create* their precursors, as for instance the Kafka of Borges creates the Browning of Borges. I mean something more drastic and (presumably) absurd, which is the triumph of having so stationed the precursor, in one's own work, that particular passages in *his* work seem to be not presages of one's own advent, but rather to be indebted to one's own achievement, and even (necessarily) to be lessened by one's greater splendor. The mighty dead return, but they return in our colors, and speaking in our voices, at least in part, at least in moments, moments that testify to our persistence, and not to their own. If they return wholly in their own strength, then the triumph is theirs:

The edges of the summit still appal
When we brood on the dead or the beloved;
Nor can imagination do it all

> In this last place of light; he dares to live
> Who stops being a bird, yet beats his wings
> Against the immense immeasurable emptiness of things.

Roethke hoped that was late Roethke, but alas it is the Yeats of *The Tower* and *The Winding Stair*. Roethke hoped this was late Roethke, but alas it is the Eliot of the *Quartets:*

> All journeys, I think, are the same:
> The movement is forward, after a few wavers,
> And for a while we are all alone,
> Busy, obvious with ourselves. . . .

There is late Roethke that is the Stevens of *Transport to Summer,* and late Roethke that is the Whitman of *Lilacs,* but sorrowfully there is very little late Roethke that is late Roethke, for in Roethke the *apophrades* came as devastation, and took away his strength, which nevertheless had been realized, which had become something of his own. Of *apophrades* in its positive, revisionary sense, he gives us no instance; there are no passages in Yeats or Eliot, in Stevens or Whitman, that can strike us as having been written by Roethke. In the exquisite squalors of Tennyson's *The Holy Grail,* as Percival rides out on his ruinous quest, we can experience the hallucination of believing that the Laureate is overly influenced by *The Waste Land,* for Eliot too became a master at reversing the *apophrades.* Or, in our present moment, the achievement of John Ashbery in his powerful poem *Fragment* (in his volume *The Double Dream of Spring*) is to return us to Stevens, somewhat uneasily to discover that at moments Stevens sounds rather too much like Ashbery, an accomplishment I might not have thought possible.

The strangeness added to beauty by the positive *apophrades* is of that kind whose best expositor was Pater.

Perhaps all Romantic style, at its heights, depends upon a successful manifestation of the dead in the garments of the living, as though the dead poets were given a suppler freedom than they had found for themselves. Contrast the Stevens of *Le Monocle de Mon Oncle* with the *Fragment* of John Ashbery, the most legitimate of the sons of Stevens:

> Like a dull scholar, I behold, in love,
> An ancient aspect touching a new mind.
> It comes, it blooms, it bears its fruit and dies.
> This trivial trope reveals a way of truth.
> Our bloom is gone. We are the fruit thereof.
> Two golden gourds distended on our vines,
> Into the autumn weather, splashed with frost,
> Distorted by hale fatness, turned grotesque.
> We hang like warty squashes, streaked and rayed,
> The laughing sky will see the two of us,
> Washed into rinds by rotting winter rains.
>
> —*Le Monocle,* VIII

> Like the blood orange we have a single
> Vocabulary all heart and all skin and can see
> Through the dust of incisions the central perimeter
> Our imaginations orbit. Other words,
> Old ways are but the trappings and appurtenances
> Meant to install change around us like a grotto.
> There is nothing laughable
> In this. To isolate the kernel of
> Our imbalance and at the same time back up carefully
> Its tulip head whole, an imagined good.
>
> —*Fragment,* XIII

An older view of influence would remark that the second of these stanzas "derives" from the first, but an awareness of the revisionary ratio of *apophrades* unveils Ashbery's relative triumph in his involuntary match with the dead. This particular strain, while it matters, is not central to Stevens, but is the greatness of Ashbery whenever, with terrible difficulty, he can win free to it. When I read *Le Monocle de Mon Oncle* now, in isolation from other poems by Stevens, I am compelled to hear Ashbery's voice, for this mode has been captured by him, inescapably and perhaps forever. When I read *Fragment,* I tend not to be aware of Stevens, for his presence has been rendered benign. In early Ashbery, amid the promise and splendors of his first volume, *Some Trees,* the massive dominance of Stevens could not be evaded, though a *clinamen* away from the master had already been evidenced:

> The young man places a bird-house
> Against the blue sea. He walks away
> And it remains. Now other
>
> Men appear, but they live in boxes.
> The sea protects them like a wall.
> The gods worship a line-drawing
>
> Of a woman, in the shadow of the sea
> Which goes on writing. Are there
> Collisions, communications on the shore
>
> Or did all secrets vanish when
> The woman left? Is the bird mentioned
> In the waves' minutes, or did the land advance?
>   —*Le Livre est sur la Table,* II

This is the mode of *The Man with the Blue Guitar,* and urgently attempts to swerve away from a vision whose severity it cannot bear:

> Slowly the ivy on the stones
> Becomes the stones. Women become
>
> The cities, children become the fields
> And men in waves become the sea.

It is the chord that falsifies.
The sea returns upon the men,

The fields entrap the children, brick
Is a weed and all the flies are caught,

Wingless and withered, but living alive.
The discord merely magnifies.

Deeper within the belly's dark,
Of time, time grows upon the rock.
        —*The Man with the Blue Guitar,* XI

The early Ashbery poem implies that there are "colli-sions, communications" among us, even in confrontation of the sea, a universe of sense that asserts its power over our minds. But the parent-poem, though it will resolve it-self in a similar quasi-comfort, harasses the poet and his readers with the intenser realization that "the discord merely magnifies," when our "collisions, communications" sound out against the greater rhythms of the sea. Where the early Ashbery attempted vainly to soften his poetic fa-ther, the mature Ashbery of *Fragment* subverts and even captures the precursor even as he appears to accept him more fully. The ephebe may still not be mentioned in the father's minutes, but his own vision has advanced. Stevens hesitated almost always until his last phase, unable firmly to adhere to or reject the High Romantic insistence that the power of the poet's mind could triumph over the uni-verse of death, or the estranged object-world. It is not every day, he says in his *Adagia,* that the world arranges itself in a poem. His nobly desperate disciple, Ashbery, has dared the dialectic of misprision so as to implore the world daily to arrange itself into a poem:

But what could I make of this? Glaze
Of many identical foreclosures wrested from

The operative hand, like a judgment but still
The atmosphere of seeing? That two people could
Collide in this dusk means that the time of
Shapelessly foraging had come undone: the space was
Magnificent and dry. On flat evenings
In the months ahead, she would remember that that
Anomaly had spoken to her, words like disjointed beaches
Brown under the advancing signs of the air.

This, the last stanza of *Fragment,* returns Ashbery full
circle to his early *Le Livre est sur la Table.* There are
"collisions, communications on the shore" but these "col-
lide in this dusk." "Did the land advance?" of the early
poem is answered partly negatively, by the brown, dis-
jointed beaches, but partly also by "the advancing signs of
the air." Elsewhere in *Fragment,* Ashbery writes: "Thus
reasoned the ancestor, and everything/Happened as he
had foretold, but in a funny kind of way." The strength of
the positive *apophrades* gives this quester the hard wis-
dom of the proverbial poem he rightly calls *Soonest
Mended,* which ends by:

> . . . learning to accept
> The charity of the hard moments as they are doled out,
> For this is action, this not being sure, this careless
> Preparing, sowing the seeds crooked in the furrow,
> Making ready to forget, and always coming back
> To the mooring of starting out, that day so long ago.

Here Ashbery has achieved one of the mysteries of po-
etic style, but only through the individuation of mispri-
sion.

The mystery of poetic style, the exuberance that is
beauty in every strong poet, is akin to the mature ego's de-
light in its own individuality, which reduces to the mys-
tery of narcissism. This narcissism is what Freud terms

primary and normal, "the libidinal complement to the egoism of the instinct of self-preservation." The strong poet's love of his poetry, *as itself,* must exclude the reality of all other poetry, except for what cannot be excluded, the initial identification with the poetry of the precursor. Any departure from initial narcissism, according to Freud, leads to development of the ego, or in our terms, every exercise of a revisionary ratio, away from identification, *is* the process generally called poetic development. If all object-libido indeed has its origin in ego-libido, then we can surmise also that each ephebe's initial experience of being found by a precursor is made possible only through an excess of self-love. *Apophrades,* when managed by the capable imagination, by the strong poet who has persisted in his strength, becomes not so much a return of the dead as a celebration of the return of the early self-exaltation that first made poetry possible.

The strong poet peers in the mirror of his fallen precursor and beholds neither the precursor nor himself but a Gnostic double, the dark otherness or antithesis that both he and the precursor longed to be, yet feared to become. Out of this deepest evasion, the complex imposture of the positive *apophrades* constitutes itself, making possible the last phases of Browning, Yeats, Stevens—all of whom triumphed against old age. *Asolando, Last Poems and Plays,* and "The Rock" section of Stevens' *Collected Poems* are all astonishing manifestations of *apophrades,* part of whose intent and effect is to make us read differently—that is, read Wordsworth, Shelley, Blake, Keats, Emerson, and Whitman differently. It is as though the final phase of great modern poets existed neither for last affirmations of a lifetime's beliefs, nor as palinodes, but rather as the ultimate placing and reduction of ancestors. But this takes us to the central problem of *apophrades:* is there still an anxiety of style as distinct from the anxiety of influence, or are the two anxieties now one? If this book's argument is correct, then the covert subject of most poetry for the last three centuries has been the anxiety of influence, each poet's fear that no proper work remains for him to perform. Clearly, there has been an anxiety of style as long as there have been literary standards. But we have seen the concept of influence (and poets' attendant morale) alter with the post-Enlightenment dualism. Did the anxiety of style change also even as the anxiety of influence began? Was the burden of individuating a style, now intolerable for all new poets, so massive a burden before the anxiety of influence developed? When we open a first volume of verse these days, we listen to hear a distinctive voice, if we can, and if the voice is not already somewhat differentiated from its precursors and its fellows, then we tend to stop listening, no matter what the voice is attempting to *say*. Dr. Samuel Johnson had an acute apprehension of the anxiety of influence, yet he still read any new poet by the test of asking whether any new matter had been disclosed. Loathing Gray, Johnson nevertheless was compelled to the highest praise of Gray on encountering notions that seemed to him original:

> The *Church-yard* abounds with images which find a mirrour in every mind, and with sentiments to which every bosom returns an echo. The four stanzas beginning *Yet even these bones,* are to me original: I have never seen the notions in any other place; yet he that reads them here, persuades himself that he has always felt them. Had Gray written often thus, it had been vain to blame, and useless to praise him.

Original *notions* which every reader has *felt,* or is persuaded he has felt; this is more difficult than the fame of

Johnson's passage allows us to see. Was Johnson accurate in finding these stanzas original?

> Yet even these bones from insult to protect
> Some frail memorial still erected nigh,
> With uncouth rhymes and shapeless sculpture decked,
> Implores the passing tribute of a sigh.

> Their name, their years, spelt by the unlettered muse,
> The place of fame and elegy supply:
> And many a holy text around she strews,
> That teach the rustic moralist to die.

> For who to dumb Forgetfulness a prey,
> This pleasing anxious being, e'er resigned,
> Left the warm precincts of the cheerful day,
> Nor cast one longing lingering look behind?

> On some fond breast the parting soul relies,
> Some pious drops the closing eye requires;
> Ev'n from the tomb the voice of nature cries,
> Ev'n in our ashes live their wonted fires.

Swift, Pope's *Odyssey,* Milton's Belial, Lucretius, Ovid, and Petrarch are all among Gray's precursors here, for as an immensely learned poet, Gray rarely wrote without deliberately relating himself to nearly every possible literary ancestor. Johnson was an immensely learned critic; why did he praise these stanzas for an originality they do not possess? A possible answer is that Johnson's own deepest anxieties are openly expressed in this passage, and to find a contemporary saying what one feels even more deeply than he does, and yet what one is inhibited from expressing oneself, is to be persuaded of more originality than exists. Gray's stanzas cry out for just that minimal and figurative immortality that the anxiety of influence denies us. Whenever the rugged Johnsonian sensibility finds fresh matter in literature, it is a safe assumption that Johnsonian repression is also involved in such finding. But, as Johnson is so universal a reader, he illustrates a tendency in many other readers, which is to be found most decisively by the notions we evade in our own minds. Johnson, who hated Gray's style, understood that in Gray's poetry the anxiety of style and the anxiety of influence had become indistinguishable, yet he forgave Gray for the one passage where Gray universalized the anxiety of self-preservation into a more general pathos. Writing on his poor friend, Collins, Johnson has Gray in mind when he observes: "He affected the obsolete when it was not worthy of revival; and he puts his words out of the common order, seeming to think, with some later candidates for fame, that not to write prose is certainly to write poetry." Johnson seems to have so compounded the burden of originality and the problem of style, that he could denounce style he judged vicious, and mean by the denunciation that no fresh matter was offered. So, despite seeming our opposite, when we neglect content and search for individuality of tone in a new poet, Johnson is very much our ancestor. By the 1740's, at the latest, the anxiety of style and the comparatively recent anxiety of influence had begun a process of merging that seems to have culminated during our last few decades.

We can see the same merger gradually manifesting itself in the pastoral elegy and its descendants, for in a poet's lament for his precursor, or more frequently for another poet of his own generation, the poet's own deepest anxieties tend to be uncovered. Moschus, lamenting Bion, begins by declaring that poetry is dead because "he is dead, the beautiful singer":

> Ye nightingales that lament among the thick
> leaves of the trees, tell ye to the Sicilian waters
> of Arethusa the tidings that Bion the herdsman is

dead, and that with Bion song too has died, and perished hath
   the Dorian minstrelsy.
   Begin, ye Sicilian Muses, begin the dirge.

   Well before *The Lament for Bion* is over, Moschus has
made the necessarily happy discovery that all song has not
died with Bion:

   . . . but I sing thee the dirge of an Ausonian sorrow,
I that am no stranger to the pastoral song, but heir of
the Doric Muse which thou didst teach thy pupils. This
was thy gift to me; to others didst thou leave thy wealth, to
   me thy minstrelsy.
   Begin, ye Sicilian Muses, begin the dirge.

   The great pastoral elegies, indeed all major elegies for
poets, do not express grief but center upon their compos-
ers' own creative anxieties. They offer therefore as conso-
lation their own ambitions (*Lycidas, Thyrsis*), or if they
are beyond ambition (*Adonais,* Whitman's *Lilacs,* Swin-
burne's *Ave Atque Vale*) then they offer oblivion. For the
largest irony of the revisionary ratio of *apophrades* is that
the later poets, confronting the imminence of death, work
to subvert the immortality of their precursors, as though
any one poet's afterlife could be metaphorically prolonged
at the expense of another's. Even Shelley, in the sublimely
suicidal *Adonais,* a poem frighteningly transcending mere
disinterestedness, subtly divests Keats of the heroic natu-
ralism that is Keats's unique gift. Adonais becomes part of
a Power that works to transform a nature considered
"dull" and "dense" by the Orphic Shelley. Keats's delight
in the natural Intelligences that are Atoms of Perception,
that know and see and therefore *are* God, becomes instead
an impatience with the unwilling dross that would check
the Spirit's flight. Shelley, in his attitude towards precur-
sors and contemporaries, was by far the most generous

strong poet of the post-Enlightenment, but even in him the final phase of the dialectic of misprision had to work itself out.

British and American poetry, at least since Milton, has been a severely displaced Protestantism, and the overtly devotional poetry of the last three hundred years has been therefore mostly a failure. The Protestant God, insofar as He was a Person, yielded His paternal role for poets to the blocking figure of the Precursor. God the Father, for Collins, is John Milton, and Blake's early rebellion against Nobodaddy is made complete by the satiric attack upon *Paradise Lost* that is at the centre of *The Book of Urizen* and that hovers, much more uneasily, all through the cosmology of *The Four Zoas*. Poetry whose hidden subject is the anxiety of influence is naturally of a Protestant temper, for the Protestant God always seems to isolate His children in the terrible double bind of two great injunctions: "Be like Me" and "Do not presume to be too like Me."

The fear of godhood is pragmatically a fear of poetic strength, for what the ephebe enters upon, when he begins his life cycle as a poet, is in every sense a process of divination. The young poet, Stevens remarked, is a god, but he added that the old poet is a tramp. If godhood consisted only in knowing accurately what is going to happen next, then every contemporary Sludge would be a poet. But what the strong poet truly knows is only that *he* is going to happen next, that he is going to write a poem in which his radiance will be manifest. When a poet beholds his end, however, he needs some more rugged evidence that his past poems are not what skeletons think about, and he searches for evidences of election that will fulfill his precursors' prophecies by fundamentally re-creating those prophecies in his own unmistakeable idiom. This is the curious magic of the positive *apophrades*.

Yeats, whose ghostly intensities of the final phase are mixed with a disinterested enthusiasm for violence, violence largely for its own sake, succeeded brilliantly in making the dead return in his idiom:

> Beneath, the billows having vainly striven
> Indignant and impetuous, roared to feel
> The swift and steady motion of the keel.
>
> . . . . . .
>
> But she in the calm depths her way could take,
> Where in bright bowers immortal forms abide
> Beneath the weltering of the restless tide.
>
> . . . . . .
>
> And she unwound the woven imagery
>   Of second childhood's swaddling bands, and took
> The coffin, its last cradle, from its niche,
> And threw it with contempt into a ditch.

We feel, in reading *The Witch of Atlas,* that Shelley has read too deeply in Yeats, and is doomed never to get the tonal complexities of the Byzantium poems out of his mind. We encounter the same phenomenon here:

> Insect lover of the sun,
> Joy of thy dominion!
> Sailor of the atmosphere;
> Swimmer through the waves of air;
> Voyager of light and noon;
> Epicurean of June;
> Wait, I prithee, till I come
> Within earshot of thy hum,—
> All without is martyrdom.

All without is martyrdom—certainly this ought to be Dickinson, but it is Emerson's *The Humble-Bee* (a poem for which Dickinson admitted some fondness). Examples abound; the hugely idiosyncratic Milton shows the influence, in places, of Wordsworth; Wordsworth and Keats both have a tinge of Stevens; the Shelley of *The Cenci* derives from Browning; Whitman appears at times too enraptured by Hart Crane. It is important only that we learn to distinguish this phenomenon from its aesthetic opposite, the embarrassment, say, of reading *The Scholar-Gipsy* and *Thyrsis,* and finding the odes of Keats crowding out poor Arnold. Keats can seem a touch over-affected by Tennyson and the Pre-Raphaelites, even by Pater, but never does he seem the heir of Matthew Arnold.

"Let the dead poets make way for others. Then we might even come to see that it is our veneration for what has already been created . . . that petrifies us. . . ." Mad Artaud carried the anxiety of influence into a region where influence and its counter-movement, misprision, could not be distinguished. If latecomer poets are to avoid following him there, they need to know that the dead poets will not consent to make way for others. But, it is more important that new poets possess a richer knowing. The precursors flood us, and our imaginations can die by drowning in them, but no imaginative life is possible if such inundation is wholly evaded. In Wordsworth's dream of the Arab, the vision of a drowning world brings no initial terror, but a prior vision of dessication immediately does. Ferenczi in his apocalypse, *Thalassa: A Theory of Genitality,* explains all myths of deluge as a reversal:

> The first and foremost danger encountered by organisms which were all originally water-inhabiting was not that of inundation but of dessication. The raising of Mount Ararat out of the waters of the flood would thus be not only a deliverance, as told in the Bible, but at the same time the orig-

inal catastrophe which may have only later on been recast from the standpoint of land-dwellers.

Artaud, desperately seeking to raise his Ararat, is at least a poignant figure; the rabblement of his disciples remind us only that we but live, as Yeats said, where motley is worn. Our poets who are capable still of unfolding in their strength live where their precursors have lived for three centuries now, under the shadow of the Covering Cherub.

EPILOGUE

Reflections upon the Path

Riding three days and nights he came upon the place, but decided it could not be come upon.

He paused therefore to consider.

This must be the place. If I have come upon it, then I am of no consequence.

Or this cannot be the place. There is then no consequence, but I am myself not diminished.

Or this may be the place. But I may not have come upon it. I may have been here always.

Or no one is here, and I am merely of and in the place. And no one can come upon it.

This may not be the place. Then I am purposeful, of consequence, but have not come upon it.

But this must be the place. And since I cannot come upon it, I am not I, I am not here, here is not here.

After riding three days and nights he failed to come to the place, and rode out again.

Was it that the place knew him not, or failed to find him? Was he not capable?

In the story it only says one need come upon the place.

Riding three days and nights he came upon the place, but decided it could not be come upon.